More about Writing

More about Writing

Designing Student Assignments with Specific Steps

Anna J. Small Roseboro

ROWMAN & LITTLEFIELD
Lanham • Boulder • New York • London

Published by Rowman & Littlefield
An imprint of The Rowman & Littlefield Publishing Group, Inc.
4501 Forbes Boulevard, Suite 200, Lanham, Maryland 20706
www.rowman.com

6 Tinworth Street, London SE11 5AL, United Kingdom

Copyright © 2019 by Anna J. Small Roseboro

All rights reserved. No part of this book may be reproduced in any form or by any electronic or mechanical means, including information storage and retrieval systems, without written permission from the publisher, except by a reviewer who may quote passages in a review.

British Library Cataloguing in Publication Information Available

Library of Congress Cataloging-in-Publication Data

Names: Roseboro, Anna J. Small, 1945- author.
Title: More about writing : designing student assignments with specific steps / Anna J. Small Roseboro.
Description: Lanham, Maryland : Rowman & Littlefield, 2019. | Includes bibliographical references.
Identifiers: LCCN 2018043056 (print) | LCCN 2018055587 (ebook) | ISBN 9781475842814 (electronic) | ISBN 9781475842791 (cloth : alk. paper) | ISBN 9781475842807 (pbk. : alk. paper)
Subjects: LCSH: English language—Composition and exercises—Study and teaching (Secondary) | English language—Rhetoric—Study and teaching (Secondary) | Creative writing (Secondary education)
Classification: LCC LB1631 (ebook) | LCC LB1631 .R615 2019 (print) | DDC 808/.0420712—dc23
LC record available at https://lccn.loc.gov/2018043056

∞™ The paper used in this publication meets the minimum requirements of American National Standard for Information Sciences—Permanence of Paper for Printed Library Materials, ANSI/NISO Z39.48-1992.

To my husband, William Gerald Roseboro, who supports me personally as I travel this professional road, and to the myriad mentors, cordial colleagues, fond friends, and faithful family members who encourage, advise, and cheer me on.

To Dr. Sandra Gibbs, who challenged me to speak up and speak out.

To teachers of teachers who include my books among their resources for preparing our next generation of professional educators.

Contents

Foreword ix

Acknowledgments xi

Introduction xiii

1 Plan Now to Be Effective and Efficient 1

2 Cultivate a Community of Writers 11

3 Explore Grammars: Traditional and Contemporary 25

4 Think on Paper: Writing in the Content Areas 35

5 Tell It Like It Is: Inviting Informative Writing 47

6 Make the Case: Writing to Impact Thinking and Acting 71

7 Verse Life Together: Reading and Writing Poetry 91

8 Entertain and Explore Life: Writing Short Stories 107

9 Dramatize It Write: Reviewing Drama and Drafting One-Act Plays 123

10 Write for Public Speaking and Media 137

Afterword 149

Bibliography 151

About the Author 153

Foreword

Writing is a means of expressing, exploring, and expanding our understanding.

—Anna J. Small Roseboro

As a teacher educator, I have the awesome privilege of teaching the next generation of educators—ones who will influence classrooms full of young learners for many years to come. With this privilege comes the responsibility to teach them what they need to know about content, methods, and especially working with diverse populations of students. Literacy learning reaches across disciplines and is much bigger than simply reading and writing. How do I best prepare teacher candidates to think critically about curriculum while supporting their students' learning needs? The short answer—find an amazing resource to use in our university classes.

In previous semesters, our texts for the middle-grade writing pedagogy class had been interesting but lacked critical information on how to align literacy lessons with curriculum standards. Five years ago, in an effort to change the focus of the class from imagining writing workshop possibilities to more concrete methods of instruction backed by common core state standards, I found Roseboro's text *Teaching Writing in the Middle School: Common Core and More*. Contained in this book was the information my teacher candidates needed to be effective writing teachers in middle-grade literacy and content classroom.

Now, as we head toward this century's third decade and ever-evolving global literacy, my students and I need a text filled with current ideologies about writing and writing instruction while maintaining reasonable and practical strategies for use in the middle school. Having used Roseboro's previous writing instruction text, *Teaching Writing in the Middle School*, I found the updated book *More about Writing: Designing Student Assignments with Specific Steps* to have maintained a foundation of literacy strategies that actually work in real classrooms while also including new information and techniques for incorporating digital literacy into writing curriculum.

From the introduction where Anna Roseboro writes of her personal experiences in teaching middle-grade students to read with writing in mind, to her ideas for being "effective and efficient" in year-long curriculum planning, into her admonitions for teachers to not only take care of their students' needs but also take care of themselves, and on through her brilliant ideas about how to *actually* teach students what they need to know while being guided by proven writing pedagogy, this was THE current writing instruction book my students and I needed.

This practical, accessible text allowed my students and me to immerse ourselves in literacy instruction—with creativity encouraged! No longer were my teacher candidates asking how writing workshop ideas could work for middle grades. Instead, they excitedly exchanged ideas in group planning times and class share-outs about how they could and would use Roseboro's suggestions. As a class, they gained confidence in themselves and their abilities to be literacy teachers. As a teacher educator, I knew this book was the one for which I had been searching. *More about Writing* is a gem of a resource and one my students and I highly recommend.

Karen Kleppe Graham, PhD
Assistant Professor
Arkansas State University
Department of Teacher Education

Acknowledgments

Teaching is both a vocation and avocation, a gift from God that I must share. Wrapping this gift is a circle of staunch friends and colleagues. Among those critical to preparing this updated edition of my 2013 book on writing are Claudia A. Marschall, my sister-friend; Laury Isenberg, who has stood with me since we met in the San Diego Area Writing Project and later taught together at The Bishop's School; and Quentin Schultze, my colleague at Calvin College, who convinced and helped me to finish the first editions that have led to invitations to publish five more books for teachers!

Teachers of students in middle school through college representing diverse ethnicities in towns and cities across the nation consented to field test ideas described in this book. They sent their own reflections and students' comments, responses, and writing samples that confirm the cultural relevance of these lessons. I am especially pleased to have early career educators: Cresence Birder, José Luís Cano, Kiondre Dunham, Cassidy Earle, and Emily Espy share their insight for this book. In this circle also are mid-career and veteran teachers like Anne Brown, Audrey Spica, and Ellen Murray, who inspire me with their generosity. I am grateful to you all.

I appreciate, too, Tom Koerner and Carlie Wall, editors at Rowman & Littlefield, who expressed confidence in my work and invited me to write *MORE ABOUT WRITING*.

Introduction

> Although no one can go back and make a brand-new start,
> anyone can start from now and make a brand-new ending.
>
> —Anonymous

Teaching students to read with writing in mind, to write for academic and personal purposes, to write just to learn, and to talk intelligently about writing need not be the overwhelming task it poses for some teachers. You may be a recent graduate, an experienced teacher transitioning from elementary or high school classrooms, or a graduate student teaching introductory writing courses while completing your own study toward an advanced degree.

You may feel challenged to design lessons for which students write regularly for real audiences but are reticent, not yet sure how to do this without burdensome grading that can wear down early career educators and veterans alike. This need not be the reality for you.

MORE ABOUT WRITING (*MAW*): Designing student assignments with specific steps describes ways to:

- establish a nurturing classroom environment with firm but fair grading guidelines;
- plan writing assignments that include strategies to adopt or adapt to your own classes; and
- balance student choice within teacher control.

Here are:

- samples of formative and summative assessments measuring student growth in writing;

- ways to select relevant texts that serve as inspiration for living and patterns for writing; and
- lessons designed to engage students from various cultural, ethnic, and economic populations across the nation.

Most important, here are ideas to help you manage the load by sharing the burden.

As a National Board Certified Teacher vetted by the National Board for Professional Teaching Standards, a National Writing Project Fellow, codirector and mentor of the National Council of Teachers of English Early Career Educators Leadership Award program for ten years, and a Literacy Center of West Michigan–trained adult English Language Learners tutor, I remain current regarding the issues facing educators teaching students born in the twenty-first century. I bring to this writing an amalgamation of my teaching and learning experiences.

Personal experiences guide my writing. I have taught in five states—California, Massachusetts, Michigan, Missouri, and New York—in urban, suburban, public, private, and parochial schools, middle school through college graduate classes, and mentored early career educators across the nation.

Sixteen years as director of summer sessions for students of grades five to twelve and five years as English Department chair instill a broad view of how knowledge and skill in teaching writing for different purposes and across content areas benefit writing teachers no matter the ages of their students. I have observed the challenges of teachers committed to their students' success. This book reflects what I learned in these roles.

Insight from these experiences has been expanded through active membership in local, state, and national professional organizations for educators, as well as serving in a variety of elected and appointed positions, including president of the California Association of Teachers of English and several roles in the Conference on English Leadership. Participants in interactive workshops I presented based on the lessons described here in *MAW* let me know there is hunger for this knowledge and experience.

College professors find *MAW* ideas useful for preparing and supporting educators who teach middle school, high school, or community college students. These teachers benefit as they explore ideas related to selecting texts and planning engaging lessons while managing grades, varying class activities, and using time efficiently with students new to the challenges in more demanding academic settings.

The progression of lessons reflects the philosophy of gradual release of responsibility. In this pedagogical approach, the teacher models spiraling steps in the writing process: drafting, giving and receiving feedback, revising, and editing. Thoughtful teachers plan in-class small group and independent practice *before* assuming students can work independently on writing tasks that assure the teacher that they can meet writing standards and learning goals for the course.

Most important, *MAW* describes ways teachers can include writing to learn and reflect on learning. From the philosophical stance, all writing does *not* have to be read and/or graded by the teacher. Here you will see effective and efficient ways to manage class time and assess student writing as they use it to inform, argue, persuade, and entertain or just to explore, explain, and expand their thinking about literature, life, and lessons learned in your course.

Yes, several texts are on the market that address issues of teaching writing in English language arts courses designed for young adolescents and preservice methods classes for literacy in the content areas. But few texts address teaching the students in ways that incorporate a map to manage the load for coaching students to write in different modes, and experience various genres of fiction and nonfiction, nor texts that narrate guided steps for class management and grading, suggesting model texts all in one book.

While most College of Education programs across the nation offer credentialing programs structured to prepare to teach in elementary schools or high schools, few have coursework designed specifically to prepare for teaching students in the middle school, freshmen in high school, or introductory community college classes. This book and the companion website, www.teachingenglishlanguagearts.com, can help fill those gaps.

Therefore, I invite you to consider the steps that can guide and coach and support and sustain you along this professional career path and enable you to become and remain an engaged, enthusiastic, and effective teacher of writing in the middle school and beyond. Explore ideas to develop and present lessons that meet students' emotional and intellectual needs while challenging them to complete increasingly complex tasks.

When students are learning, and you can document that learning through appropriate assessments, both you and your students enjoy more of your time together on the journey of a school year. Here in *MORE ABOUT WRITING* you may discover ideas and expand your instruction options with practical and proven practices that bring you the kind of pleasure in teaching and mentoring early career educators that I have experienced for more than four decades.

Chapter 1

Plan Now to Be Effective and Efficient

> The mediocre teacher tells.
> The good teacher explains.
> The superior teacher demonstrates.
> The great teacher inspires.
>
> —William A. Ward[1]

Teaching writing can drain one's time and energy, but intentional planning can help you use both more efficiently and effectively. Four of the more time-consuming tasks of teaching are figuring out how to use class time productively, managing grades, providing feedback on student writing, and incorporating technology that supports rather than thwarts learning. But few of these challenges will improve much if you have not taken time to scope out the year and make some general plans to get to know your students each school year.

It may seem odd, but a good place to begin planning and personalizing instruction for a whole school year is to focus on school holidays, breaks, and vacations. Aha! You recall from your own days as a student how challenging it was to be attentive the few days before and after any of these three! Among the ways you can assure your teaching stays on course is by planning assignments that maximize instruction on potentially lost days.

At one school where I taught, we had to post tests on the grade-level calendar and were forbidden to add our test if two were already scheduled that day. This required negotiations with colleagues but reduced stress for students. It

Plan with school breaks in mind

also required some preplanning to arrange summative assessments in a timely fashion to be test one or two on our preferred date.

LEARN ABOUT YOUR STUDENTS

Take into consideration ethnicities and cultures of students in your classes. What holidays do they share in common? Which are unique to a few? How can you integrate into your lessons the wealth of information, experience, and passion surrounding holidays, breaks, and vacations? Subtler to think about is the emotional and physical drain, say, on your Jewish and Muslim students who, for cultural or religious reasons, may be fasting on a day you planned to schedule a major test. Many Asian families observe their calendar new year with days of celebrations that may run late into the evening, making it difficult for students to attend to homework. What kind of reading, writing, active learning, critical thinking, and even reflection can you organize to redeem the time and channel the energy of easily distracted students?

In addition to knowing the cultures and ethnicities of your students, it is important to learn a little more about them, their families, and circumstances in which they live. How much do you know about resources available in the community where your school is located, or your students live? Are there local libraries with technology available? Once you have your class lists, take a look at any notices regarding special physical or emotional needs. Plan time to meet with support staff and paraprofessionals with whom you will share students.

What are you learning that may impact the way you set up your classroom or design lessons? In conversations with veteran teachers, what can you learn about the most efficient ways to initiate and maintain communication with families regarding languages spoken at home and their access to technology? What is required at your school? Do you have a choice to contact by phone or e-mail? Just as a tour company would gather this information before the trip begins to help ensure the safety and success of its clients, so should a teacher commit to being ready for those inherent eventualities. As in scouting, you want to be prepared.

PREPLAN WAYS TO MANAGE GRADING

In this chapter are ways to manage grading with customized rubrics and general grading guidelines. Consider starting with these ideas that can revolutionize your planning and grading for teaching middle, high school, and college students.

CUSTOMIZED RUBRICS

After you have considered what students are expected to know and be able to do in terms of writing by the end of the school year, develop or adapt a general rubric, like the Six Traits rubric published by the Education Northwest and available online. That original rubric had descriptive statements relating to *ideas, organization, voice, word choice, sentence fluency*, and *conventions*; recent charts have added *presentation*. All are writing traits you will measure at the end of the course. Share the rubric at the beginning of the school year and customize it for specific assignments.

- For example, for ideas in content, when students are writing about fiction, you may require that they include references and/or quotations from

the beginning, middle, and end of the assigned reading. Or if students are doing research, customize the rubric for that assignment and add that for maximum credit students must include evidence from three to five different kinds of sources.
- For word choice, you may customize your rubric and require students to use literary terms correctly, incorporate eight to ten words from a current vocabulary list, or weave quotations seamlessly into their own writing.
- In terms of conventions, after teaching students how to cite sources, add to your rubric words like "includes a bibliography and punctuates quotations correctly." For young or inexperienced writers, you may find that page numbers in parentheses and alphabetized lists of sources consulted will suffice early in the year. Older, more experienced students should be required to use endnotes and construct bibliographies in the style used at your school or institution.

Before you review or teach a skill, there is no need to mark students down for not exhibiting that feature. Use the same general rubric all year long; then once a trait is reviewed, modeled, and practiced, customize that rubric, reminding students that their grades now will reflect their skill at exhibiting that trait and using that convention correctly.

GENERAL GRADING GUIDELINES

Sharing with students a chart with general grading guidelines, as shown in figure 1.1, reduces both angst and challenges to grades. Let students know how they can earn a C, B, and A on big assignments, especially those that can make or break a grade. Grading also becomes less stressful when you understand what you are looking for in each assignment and share these expectations with the students. They can review their work before turning it in, using your guidelines as a checklist. Some students, because of other commitments, may settle for a B rather than put in the time to earn the A. That's okay. It is their choice.

Fewer students challenge their grades when they have had a clearly written set of printed instructions to which they can refer before submitting their work. Explain these guidelines in the first couple of weeks but not on the first day of school. Students already will be overwhelmed with the

GENERAL GRADING GUIDELINES

A = complete, correct, and creative
B = complete and correct
C = complete
D = deficient (something missing)
F = failing, for now

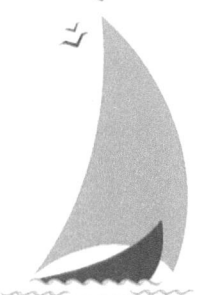

C = THE SEA – *Complete* (include all components of the assignment)
B = THE BOAT - Complete and *correct* (rides on the sea with minimal errors in mechanics, usage, grammar, and spelling)
A = THE SAIL - Complete, correct, and *creative* (something over and beyond the boat; original and fresh elements enhancing the final written paper, performance, digital or art product)

Figure 1.1. Share grading guidelines with students, parents, and administrators
Source: Liubov Trapeznykova

newness of everything! You can, however, have something like the following posted on your website and on any general handouts you distribute on opening day.

C = Complete (includes all components of the assignment)
B = Complete and Correct (minimal errors in mechanics, usage, grammar, and spelling)
A = Complete, Correct, and Creative (something original, fresh, special that enhances final paper, performance, or product)

When you include the customized rubric with assignments, students can do a self-check before submitting assignments for grading. These customized rubrics also come in handy for those in-class and online peer feedback assignments that are crucial in the writing process described in lessons in this book. See textbox 1.1 for one basic structure that, after comfortably used in class, can be adapted for homework if students have Internet access at home.

TEXTBOX 1.1

PEER COMMENTS ON CLASSMATES' DRAFTS

Find your name on the class list.

1. Skip SIX names on the list.
2. Upload the drafts of the next students.
3. Save to desktop with Last Name—A, Last Name—B, and Last Name—C.
4. Upload comments to DISCUSSION BOARD using REPLY function. Put COMMENDATION AND RECOMMENDATION in message BOX.

For *Classmate A*—Read and insert comments on general content. Consider the body of the writing.

- Best organization pattern (text structure)
- Variety of support information

Comment on strengths. Ask questions that arise as you read.

For *Classmate B*—Read and insert comments on general structure. Consider Introduction.

- Credibility mentioned?
- Thesis/signpost?

Consider transitions within the body of the writing.

- Do they fit the organization pattern identified?
- Does writer cite sources within the text?
- Check the domains. Correct format.

Comment on strengths. Ask questions that arise as you read.

For *Classmate C*—Read and insert comments on visual aids and references.

- Consider what and where the writer plans to use visual aids.
- Consider the quality and variety of the references.
- Does writer cite sources within the outline?
- Check the domains.
- Correct format (alpha order hanging indent).

Comment on strengths. Ask questions that arise as you read.

GRADUALLY INCREASE WEIGHT OF ASSIGNMENTS

At the start of the year, big assignments (processed papers and projects on which students have time to plan, get peer feedback, and revise) need not be weighted heavily enough to "kill" a report card grade. Similar high standards can be expected for early assignments; students who have time to see the standards and get feedback on their performance are seldom so discouraged that they stop trying. You may plan about 500 points per marking period. Daily work completed on time earns full credit. Regular check-up quizzes graded in class by students can be worth 10–50 points. Both daily writing and sporadic quizzes serve as practice for them and formative assessments for you.

For example:

- First quarter: 2–3 processed papers/projects/presentations = 30 points each
- Second quarter: 2–3 processed papers/projects/presentations = 50 points each
- Third quarter: 1–2 processed papers/projects/presentations = 75 points each
- Fourth quarter: 1–2 processed papers/projects/presentations = 100 points each

Student talk teaches. Lessons in upcoming chapters describe several ways to conduct no-stress assessments as students talk with partners and in small groups as they prepare to write. As you gain more understanding of the value of planning and presenting speeches to get students thinking about audience, and you become more confident evaluating oral presentations, you may find yourself adapting more of these oral strategies.

Include multimedia presentations often as they are an authentic way for students to practice what you are teaching and for you to measure that learning. They are a terrific way for students to learn from one another while developing a skill they will need for a lifetime. A sample schedule to manage and grade a week of speeches is in chapter 10, "Write for Public Speaking and Media," as well as a sample feedback form.

PREPPING STUDENTS TO USE NEW ELECTRONIC DEVICES AND PROGRAMS

It is easy to assume that students already are tech savvy and can easily use the equipment or the computer programs available at your school. But stop a minute: recall the small snags that frustrated you when you first used a new electronic device, a new computer program, or an application.

Ask the tech rep to help you design lessons to show students efficient ways to navigate the technology available and give you some basic troubleshooting

Structure in-class peer feedback

techniques when—not if—they arise. You can get off to a smoother start if you anticipate and prepare to address four basic steps. For students new to the school, you may need to help them learn how to:

- turn on the device;
- log in using their school ID;

- create a password (some schools have specific requirements for passwords); and
- navigate the specific program for doing their first assignment.

Prepare for a class demonstration during the second week of school with:
- a protocol for getting out and putting away the tablets or electronic devices;
- a class list with student school-assigned login names and general password;
- a printed handout with steps to access the school portal leading to the program for just the first assignment (avoid overload and introduce other programs at a later date);
- slides that demonstrate key steps for each of these tasks (save for later reviews);
- a short video tutorial that reviews the steps for using the program. Check online;
- screenshots showing what students should see on their devices when they get to specific steps in the program;
- a short assignment to complete during the class period. This could be sending you an e-mail with "HELLO from Period #" in the subject

Support in-class instruction with safe websites

line and, in the body of the e-mail, three things they hope to learn this school year; and
- a timer to ring ten minutes before class ends, to allot time for students to log off and for you to collect and store equipment/devices for the next period.

Circulate and assist as needed. If you have students familiar with the technology, invite them to be teaching assistants for the day. By preparing and accepting help, you can reduce the frustration of getting students online, into the school portal, and having a successful experience.

CONCLUSION

Various ways to schedule and implement in-class and online peer feedback are described in upcoming chapters on writing to learn, to inform, to persuade, and to entertain. For now, move on to ways to organize lessons for the opening days of class. They are designed to begin the journey with students and teachers getting to know and trust one another enough to write freely and give courteous and constructive feedback, while learning with and from each other as each of you develop as a writer, speaker, and consumer of media. Yes, teaching is another way of learning.

NOTE

1. "William Arthur Ward," *Brainy Quotes*. https://www.brainyquote.com/quotes/william_arthur_ward_103463 (accessed June 29, 2018).

Chapter 2

Cultivate a Community of Writers

> Getting to know you,
> getting to know all about you.
> Getting to like you,
> getting to hope you like me.
>
> —Oscar Hammerstein[1]

Even in the age of electronic social networking, in-person relationships are the most meaningful for teachers and learners. The classroom itself is a "site" for social networking among increasingly diverse students and teachers. You know how important it is to prime the pump, increase the flow of ideas, and ready students to explore, explain, and express themselves on the journey to come. You may have planned a couple activities for the first days of school to help your students get to know one another and you, both online and in the classroom. Now, how about considering an alternate plan based on names? They best show who we are and ways we may have developed as learners.

EXPLORING AND WRITING ABOUT NAMES

> We must wear our names within all the noise and confusion of the environment in which we find ourselves; make them the center of all our associations with the world, with man and with nature. We must charge them with all our emotions, our hopes, hates, loves, aspirations. They must become our masks and our shields, and the containers of all those values and traditions which we learn and/or imagine as being the meaning of our familial past.
>
> —Ralph Ellison, "Hidden Name and Complex Fate"[2]

Learn their names

Names are important. They can distinguish one thing from another and link a person to families, cultures, and communities. Names can make students proud or embarrassed, one with others, and separate from others. This paradox of emotions poses a challenge and an opportunity. This paradox makes for an engaging unit in communication, culture, and identity that incorporates lessons that can help establish a community of supportive writers who know about one another; they become willing to share their writing and exchange feedback with classmates.

Depending on your school district, your eighth or ninth graders may be the oldest, youngest, or only students on campus. In any setting, they are in their early teens, eager to become independent of their parents or guardians, often straining against the ties that bind them. These adolescents are developing their own self-identities distinct from that of their families. That often is true of older students, too.

This assignment provides opportunities for students of all ages to rekindle fond relationships with their families and talk about their names. These lessons require students to consult their parents or other family members to complete some of the assignments in this unit of study. Family members may recall their own warm memories of choosing a name for their child, and for a few days both older and younger ones can bask in that warmth.

Writing about living with a name is an interesting way to learn a little more about your students. Whether they have been together for several years or are just meeting each other for the first time, this assignment builds a more trusting learning community in a nonthreatening way. Perhaps it is because the students will be doing what so many teens like to do best—talking about themselves!

Alerting You with Words of Caution

Talking about names can cause emotional difficulties for some students and their families. You must be sensitive to the fact that some students are unable to get the information for this project for personally traumatic reasons. If you learn that any of your students do not live with parents or do not communicate regularly with their parents or family members, just modify the assignment so these young people can complete it without appearing uncooperative or inept.

Consider the ethnicities of your students. When children are in elementary school, their social studies assignments sometimes require that students trace their history and create and display their family trees. This proves to be difficult or impossible for many students. Because of the practice of chattel slavery in the United States, few African Americans know their family's genealogy; they cannot even talk without anguish about their ancestry.

Prior to the 1860s, the birth records of African Americans included few surnames and, when kept at all, first names often were recorded among the cattle records. Even in the twenty-first century, few African Americans could trace their ancestry more than a few generations. Those families that can trace their history may already know that they carry the names of those slave owners. Most know that their families originated on the continent of Africa, but few have access to information that can verify the country or the tribe.

Discussing the issue of ancestry proves to be difficult for some students and impossible for others. This may be the case for current new-to-America students whose families may have come to escape political unrest in their country of origin. Clearly you know to avoid any name-tracing assignments that may cause undue anxiety for students and families. The more diverse your school's community, the more careful you may need to be. You could redesign the project so the final writings can be based on real or imagined incidents.

If you teach in a community with a large number of immigrants from war-torn countries, you may discover that some families are able but unwilling to discuss their lineage. Ancestors may have changed their names to protect themselves from political repercussions. On the other hand, such families may appreciate the fact that you are interested in learning more about their cultures and are thrilled with the opportunity to share theirs.

Be similarly on the alert to situations with blended families in which parents and siblings have different last names and when students have blended or hyphenated names. Know that in some cultures, children have different names from those of their parents simply because it is part of their traditions. A teacher new to the school or community knows to confer with veterans at the school and then adapt the unit as needed to gain the benefits and avoid the pitfalls.

With this many pitfalls, why bother? Because just reading literature about naming and living with names can be a rich, intellectual experience for your students! In addition, the accompanying assignments help meet several typical curriculum standards for English language arts in interesting and illuminating ways. The following unit includes lessons for:

- reading, discussing, and analyzing literary works in a variety of genres;
- learning name-related vocabulary;
- conducting various kinds of research (online, library, and interview);
- writing short essays, vignettes, autobiographical sketches, and giving oral reports;
- composing short stories patterned after literary works read; and
- participating in peer editing groups.

Selecting Literary Works about Names

Begin with an overview of a lesson you can call simply "What's in a Name?" One very popular name-related assignment is based on Sandra Cisneros's "My Name," a chapter from *House on Mango Street*, her autobiographical vignette about growing up as a child of Mexican immigrants in Chicago.

As you get to know your students and plan your unit, you can add or substitute other name-related narratives. This can include stories and poems about various ethnic or cultural groups reflecting your school population, determined each year by the reading level of current students. Three selections that seem most accessible to all students are Cisneros's vignette "My Name"; Santha Rama Rau's autographical sketch "By Any Other Name," set in British colonial India; and "The Name," Aharon Megged's short story set in modern Israel, describing Jewish naming traditions.

"Hidden Name and Complex Fate," a sophisticated essay by Ralph Ellison, an African American named by his father for Ralph Waldo Emerson, works incredibly well as a springboard for discussing issues of living with a name. Even if your students are not particularly strong readers, you still can begin with the Ellison essay. In that case, read it in class with support to aid understanding. Remind them that expository writing uses text structures they may have learned earlier. If necessary, do a mini-lesson introducing these structures to your students. Ellison's essay inspired the questions you can use for the students' research and writing about their own names. (See textbox 2.1.)

> **TEXTBOX 2.1**
> **RESEARCH YOUR NAMES**
>
> 1. Use a dictionary and/or online resources to find out what each of your own names means.
> 2. Interview a family member to learn the sources of your name(s). If you have equipment, audio- or videotape the interview. Who named you and why? Are you named for a friend or family member? Someone else?
> 3. Determine the kind of surname or last name you have. Is it a place name, like Al-Fassi, Hall, or Rivera; an occupation, like Chandler, Smith, or Taylor; a descriptive, Braun or Strong; or a patronymic or version of a father's name, like Ben-Yehuda, McNeil, or Von Wilhelm?
> 4. Describe incidents you have experienced because of your name, including mispronunciations, misspellings, and misunderstandings.
> 5. Write about nicknames and related embarrassing or humorous experiences.
> 6. Identify challenges you feel because of the name(s) you carry.

If you decide to extend this unit beyond the opening week, consider substituting or adding a chapter from Richard Kim's *Lost Names*, about Korean families forced by the government of Japan to adopt Japanese names; *Not Even My Name*, an autobiographical work by Thea Halo about Pontic Greeks in Turkey; or *The Namesake*, a novel by Jhumpa Lahiri, about naming traditions of a family from India. Let your own interest and that of your students guide your selections each year. As always, select readings to fit your current school setting, literature that serves as windows for seeing others and mirrors for seeing self.

Reading, Researching, and Learning Vocabulary of Names

During the first couple weeks of this four-week unit, read and analyze the literature selections to discover their organizational pattern, diction, and sentence structure. Discuss the vocabulary of naming, including the following concepts:

- surname
- given name
- nickname

Get to know them—write away

- nom de plume
- pseudonym
- pen name
- alias

The assignment prompt that asks students to interview a family member provides enough information to get them started on learning how they have come to have the names they have been given. You may need to review with young researchers the correct way to cite an interview in the text of the essay and the format for their bibliographies.

With expanded resources available on the Internet, most students are able to find enough information to fulfill the basic purposes of the assignment—to consider their own names, conduct research, and write about traditions of naming they discover. If students have uncommon names or common names that are spelled uncommonly, they may need a bit of help identifying similar, researchable alternatives. Prepare them for research by showing them alternative spellings of the same name, such as mine—Anna, Ana, Ann, Anne, Annie, Anouska, Anya, and even Hannah.

Students who have online access from home and some parental supervision of the project might benefit from using ancestry.com and similar websites to

Experiment with peer feedback options

collect historical information about their family names. By all means, share your name story and write along with your students.

As students consider responses to these prompts, they reflect on who they are in their families, the school, the wider community, and perhaps even the world. Some of the students may learn family history never previously discussed. Other students awaken tender memories of relatives and family friends for whom they have been named. Some may just be embarrassed, others pleasantly surprised.

One student developed a new appreciation for a stepfather and deepened her relationships with her biological parents. This student's first name is a combination of her biological parents' first names. Her stepfather later adopted her and she now carries his surname.

Discovering Fascinating Facts about Names

As students read about name-related experiences during peer-response sessions, they discover surprising naming traditions observed in the families of their classmates. They might learn that in some villages in India all the girls in a family may have the same middle name or that some Thai families carry extremely long, polysyllabic names, like Prachyaratanawooti, for which each syllable represents a generation the family has lived in that region. Students might learn that in some families it is the grandmother who chooses grandchildren's names, that the eldest son always is named for his father, or that the middle name for all the children is their mother's maiden name.

Your students may notice interesting combinations of Anglo and Asian or Spanish names. Some students find out that their families' names have been Americanized to avoid discrimination based on ethnicity, religion, or nationality. A number of your students may have saints' day names or hyphenated last names that include both their mother's maiden name and their father's last name. Some learn the spelling of their surnames is simply the result of an error made when their ancestors entered the country through Ellis Island in New York or Angel Island in San Francisco. No one ever bothered to correct the mistake.

One of the assignment prompts invites students to talk about the challenges of living with their names, as described in the essay by Ralph Ellison "Hidden Name and Complex Fate." Some student writing may reveal that carrying the name of a particularly famous or infamous relative causes them discomfort. One young man named for his father, a prominent businessman in the community, acknowledged in his essay that he felt unworthy to be called Robert and insisted that his peers call him Robbie, a diminutive version of the father's strong name.

Cecilia, a talented singer, was depressed for a few days on learning that the name she loves means "blind one" but then jubilant after discovering that St. Cecilia is the patron saint of music and musicians.

Other students may write about the embarrassment of having to correct the pronunciation of their name at the beginning of every school year, and the frustration of having to spell their name everywhere they go. These reminders of how sensitive students are about their names remind us to learn to pronounce and spell each student's name as early in the semester as possible. It is just another way of honoring each one as an individual with his or her own special name.

SPRINGBOARDING TO WRITING

Distribute a copy of the vignette "My Name," by Sandra Cisneros, and prepare to conduct a "jump in reading" activity to help students get a feel for the style and to think about what the writer may be "saying to them." First ask students to read silently, underlining words or phrases that catch their attention. Then you read the vignette out loud, asking students again to underline words or phrases they think are interesting or important. Finally, starting at the beginning again, invite one student to begin reading, stopping at the first mark of punctuation. Others jump in to read, without being called upon, and read to the next punctuation mark. If more than one student begins reading at the same time, urge each to listen to the other(s) and read as one voice. Between voices, let the silence resonate.

You may recall from doing this kind of reading of poetry that students are uncomfortable at first, giggle a bit, but soon catch on. The silence between the sounds of different single voices and combinations of multiple voices leaves indelible impressions and elicits powerful results in the next step of this assignment—writing.

To help the students comfortably share their stories, after reading "My Name" by Sandra Cisneros, ask them to do a "quick write" based on a phrase or sentence that they select from the vignette. A quick write is short, nonstop writing on an assigned topic. For a brief spurt of time—for example, three to seven minutes—students let their thoughts flow without censoring them. In this assignment, ask students to copy an underlined phrase or sentence from the reading. Then use that phrase or sentence as a jumping-off point to write rapidly about their own names for six or seven minutes. Write along with them. The following is a quick write based on Cisneros's piece:

A PERSONAL STORY

"My Name," A Quick Write Inspired By
Sandra Cisneros's Vignette of the Same Name

Anna Jamar Small Roseboro. Is this "me"? My name is a combination of my paternal grandmother's, Anna; my maternal grandmother's, Jamie; my dad's name, Small; and my husband's name, Roseboro. Everyone has had my name—made something of it, then passed it along to me. Anna means "gift of God." Is it I who am the gift or my grandmother who is a gift to me? Jamie is short for Jamar. My grandmother, whose full name is Jamar Elna, is named for her four aunts, Jane, Martha, Ellen and Nora—what a burden, what a privilege, to carry the names of so many relatives. Or is it a blessing? Am I standing on the shoulders of those who've come before me?

Small, my maiden name always caused me trouble. "Small," they'd tease. "You're not small; you're tall!" I was always the tallest girl in my elementary school classes. In high school, however, I used the name to my advantage. I ran for a senior class office. My slogan was "Good things come in Small packages." Finally, success with that name.

Then, I married Bill Roseboro during the years that Johnny Roseboro was a star catcher for the LA Dodgers. He'd been in the news because of a fight with Juan Marichal. Everywhere I went, "Are you related to Johnny Roseboro?" "Yes, but what has that to do with me?"

Who am I really?

EXTENDING THE EXPERIENCE OR KEEPING IT BRIEF

The extended writing assignment in this unit on names asks students to select an author's style they like and pattern that style to write about their experience of living with their own names. Some students are comfortable with the familiar, formal essay style of Ellison; others enjoy story telling with a strong sense of place in Rau's piece "By Any Other Name"; and others take on the challenge of using a series of symbols as in Megged's "The Name." Some may choose one of these genres or blend one or two.

RAG SESSIONS TO PRACTICE
GIVING AND RECEIVING PEER FEEDBACK

Choose a way to organize a class session during which students give and receive peer feedback. One you may find effective early in the school year is a read-around group (RAG) session, during which students bring a completed early draft to class and sit in circles of five or six students. First, review the sample rubric to remind students of the criteria on which their writing is to be evaluated. It may be a rubric you create together, an adaptation of one in your textbook, or one you download from the Internet.

Then, have students write their names on the rubric and lay it on top of their drafts. One student from each group collects all the drafts and hands them to you. Distribute the drafts to other groups so that none of the students in the group is reading the paper of anyone else in their group (Group A gets Group B papers, Group B gets Group C papers, etc.). This way a student is less likely to be distracted by watching how classmates respond to his or her paper. During the RAG, each student reads five or six papers but responds to only two. Do not allow those without a draft to sit in on a RAG.

Fairness suggests that paper-less students sit out and use the time to work on their drafts. First, it is useful to give those who are behind on their own writing class time to catch up. Second, if a student in a group does not have a paper to be read each round, then someone else has to "sit" out because of too few papers.

No need to worry about students coming unprepared the next time. Most are ready for the next RAG because they want to see what others have written and also want to get peer feedback and suggestions for their own revisions. Curiosity is a great motivator.

Once the groups are formed and have their stack of papers, the group leader distributes the drafts to group members, and you set a timer for three minutes, which usually is enough time to read the two to four pages of these early drafts. Students read the first paper until the timer goes off, then pass the paper to the right and read the second paper, and finally the third paper and fourth until the timer goes off again. After the fourth pass, set the timer for six minutes.

This time, the students read and comment on the content of the paper. On the fifth pass, again set the timer for six minutes, and the students read and comment on the structure and style. By this time the students have learned a great deal about their classmates; about the ways their peers have responded to the prompts; about the problems that arise when one makes mechanical, usage, grammar, and spelling errors; and, equally enlightening, about the quality of the pool of writing in which their own papers are to be read.

While students are reading the first two or three drafts, you can walk around the classroom, rubber-stamp the written drafts, and/or record in your grade book a check for the students who have their drafts ready on this due date. Afterward, during the longer reading times, you have a few moments to confer with those who have come unprepared and can offer suggestions to get them back on track with their writing.

At the end of the RAG session, each leader collects his or her group's papers and hands them to you. Return them along with the completed rubrics to the students who wrote them. Spend ten minutes or so soliciting from the students what they noticed about the strengths of their papers and invite suggested strategies for improving them.

Use the remainder of the period for students to read the comments from their peers and then to write three steps they will take to revise their papers. If time remains in the period, quickly scan and then stamp/initial the plans the students have made to improve their papers. This simply creates a record that the student has received feedback and has outlined a plan for revising. If students are doing this assignment online, remind them to save their plan in their folder. You can review them later.

Assign the students to have their final drafts ready for you in two or three days. During the intervening days, schedule in-class writing time for students to work on their revisions. Then you can meet individually with students who are not sure what steps they should take to make their next draft better.

Do not feel frustrated if you find yourself adjusting length of time needed for revision. Ask the students. If they feel confident and can quickly complete a revision they are eager to have you read, set a short deadline. If they are working diligently but believe they need more time, extend the deadline. Thankfully, students become personally invested in these papers and want you to see their best work. Do both them and yourself a favor—create a schedule that is flexible enough to allow them to revise. Well-written papers are a pleasure to read and take less time to grade.

If you teach in a setting where it is unrealistic to expect students to word process the final drafts at home, allot additional class time for students to use school equipment. Especially in writing, it is more important that students complete a few assignments well than to rush through lots of assignments they cannot finish carefully and turn in with pride. This name-writing assignment is one to which they usually are willing to devote time. Students are eager to do a good job on this paper. The subject, after all, is the students themselves.

On the due date, students should submit for evaluation a packet that includes their stamped drafts, the rubric with their plan, and the final draft stapled to the top. This stack of papers substantiates that the process of writing is a lot of work. If they have worked totally online and have done online peer reviews instead of RAGs, then students should keep and submit all drafts in a file you can view online. See chapter 6 for an online peer-response lesson.

Valuing the Writing Process and Assignment about Names

These steps in the process of drafting a paper are important for teachers, individual writers, and their classmates. Scheduling this assignment early in the school year gives you an opportunity to observe how students handle various steps in the writing process. You will expect them to be able to take these steps with relative independence by the end of the school year. Based on what you observe this opening month of school, you can design or adapt lessons appropriate for the learning of students you have in each class.

The writers get feedback during the interim stages of writing and see how peers are addressing the assignment. For many students this is both a comfort and a challenge. When they see that they and their peers are having similar problems, they do not feel so odd or incompetent. On the other hand, when they see how well some of their peers are doing, individual students realize that the task is possible, and they are challenged to work a little harder to meet the assignment's standards.

Overall, this assignment is important whether given at the beginning, middle, or end of the school year because it allows students to write from a personal perspective. During conferences, parents often express appreciation for being consulted as knowledgeable resources. What is more, this assignment creates a positive, supportive atmosphere in class.

Young adults enjoy writing about themselves and reading about each other. Perhaps most important, "What's in a Name?" enables students to complete an assignment successfully anytime you give it. You and your students get to enjoy writing that is lively and interesting. Finally, even though students may model their prose after quality published writing, they truly are developing their own, authentic voices, one of the primary goals of the English language arts standards at your school.

CONCLUSION

Seriously consider this unit as an efficient way to blend reading and writing as you work to establish a nurturing environment in which students can be both vulnerable and supporting. Names reveal much about who and whose we are, where we have been, and where we might want to be going. Generation to generation and place to place, names teach us about who we are as diverse communities. To be human is to name. To name is to be human. Naming is an art—a language art.

NOTES

1. Oscar Hammerstein, "Getting to Know You." Sound Track Lyrics. http://www.stlyrics.com/lyrics/thekingandi/gettingtoknowyou.htm (accessed June 29, 2018).
2. Ralph Ellison, "Hidden Name and Complex Fate." In *Shadow and Act* (New York: Random House, Inc., 1998), 148.

Chapter 3

Explore Grammars: Traditional and Contemporary

It is no longer an advantage to speak English, but a requirement! Just speaking English isn't so impressive anymore—unless you speak it really well.

—Heather Hansen[1]

Language is a glorious art, a phenomenal means of communication, and linguistic diversity is a gift to humankind. At the same time, there are always more formal, mainstream versions of languages that symbolize what it means to be educated. In so many areas of life, skillful use of languages leads to success in the workplace and in society, in general. This chapter explores reasons for incorporating discussions of culturally sensitive grammar and writing into your instructional practices.

In a diverse world full of different idiolects and dialects, students increasingly need to know how languages work so they can "code switch" in personal, professional, and public life. Fiction is one of the best ways to introduce students to Standard English usage so that they become more fluent in "good grammar," even as they become more amenable to other grammatical styles. Therefore, think about the ideas in the chapter as you plan lessons that help raise awareness of grammar   that set of rules that govern the structure of oral and written speech—and design activities to help your students understand the value of knowing when to use Standard English grammar to achieve academic and professional success.

CHOOSING THE RIGHT GRAMMAR

Few students and not all teachers use perfect grammar, but both groups recognize when others use it incorrectly. Even though you and your students may come from backgrounds with linguistic variations, students generally expect learned prose to sound the same—formal and correct—and see school as a place for more elevated language, not necessarily the real world as they know it outside of the classroom.

For those students who did not grow up hearing Standard English, school is a place where this different language is spoken, read, and written. This reality, then, may be a good reason to teach English dialects the same way language teachers teach English speakers to learn languages like Arabic, French, or Spanish. In order to encourage speaking the specific language, some instructors tell students that once they cross the threshold of the classroom, they are to communicate only in the language they are learning. This is pretty drastic for an English language arts class but worth considering in a modified form.

Of course, when students talk among themselves in small groups, there is no need to stop them from speaking their dialects. But in full-class discussion, urge them to code switch or code blend and incorporate as much Standard English as possible. This practice can serve them well outside the classroom when they find themselves in situations where it is personally or professionally advantageous for them to speak Standard English.

Plan weekly class day for speaking only Standard English

Your students become amenable to grammar lessons when they learn that you are teaching them a form of speaking and writing that is useful to them, not only in school but also in the broader community of college, career, business, and civic life. True, Standard English is not all there is to the real world. Still, it is essential for students of all linguistic backgrounds to learn when, where, why, and how to switch among linguistic variations. The real issue is not who speaks or writes "properly" but instead how well someone can communicate effectively in various settings. Because most students understand this, you do not need to avoid the issues of language, culture, power, and privilege. Use the issues as teaching topics that hit home, even for those from superficially homogeneous communities.

During their study of literature, students discover that some successful authors break the rules of Standard English.

Some students are shocked that Mark Twain and Toni Cade Bambara, author of "Blues Ain't No Mockingbird," does not seem to write "good grammar." You can show how authors, too, employ code-switching or code-mixing in order to lend legitimacy to characters who would seem phony if they used only Standard English grammar. Except perhaps in semi-fictional autobiography, writing fiction requires character-building code-switching.

Authors of young adult fiction who write well in other dialects include Rudolfo Anaya, Sharon Draper, Rosalinda Hernandez, Zora Neale Hurston, Barry Milliken, Walter Dean Myers, Alberto Alvara Rios, Juanita Sanchez, Gary D. Schmidt, Amy Tan, and Wing Tek. So, yes, teaching fiction is a propitious time to teach about both Standard English and the use of the dialects students may speak, hear, or read in their literature.

PRACTICING STANDARD ENGLISH

If the students you teach speak different dialects of English, you could set up a schedule for them to practice Standard English. In the first semester of the school year, after you have introduced the idea of dialects and reasons to be fluent in Standard English, you could set aside one day a week for speaking only in Standard English once the students cross the threshold into your classroom. In order to avoid silencing reluctant students and discouraging shy ones from speaking at all, commend the class for their efforts rather than correcting each one who makes an error. The second semester, you could add a second day a week. If students are amenable, during the final quarter or marking period of the school year, add a third day. As students become more fluent reading and writing Standard English in the classroom, they gain more competence and confidently use it when the need arises outside the classroom.

Occasionally, for practice in journal writing, you could require them to use specific Standard English grammatical structures and more of the sophisticated vocabulary they encounter reading the fiction and nonfiction you assign. There is no need to grade these practice entries; periodically read and just comment on their writing. In all cases, do what you can to ensure that students' own languages and dialects are never disparaged.

INTRODUCING THE GRAMMAR TEXT

Your textbook may be a viable teaching tool and can help you accomplish this goal. But do not assume that students understand the purpose of the text or that the text itself is adequate to engage students steeped in multimedia experience when you first distribute the book to students. Address the first issue by showing them how the book is organized, what it contains, and what it's for—a resource and a guide.

Address the second issue by considering not only the insights and activities in this book but also the digital resources provided by the publisher. You are the professional in the classroom, the one who knows the students and their specific needs. Even if some of the resources are impractical or excessively time-intensive tools, you still might find a few student-engaging gems.

HONORING LA DIFFÉRENCE

Inevitably the issues of dialects in reading, writing, and discussion arise when teachers require that students use Standard English texts and require Standard English–based assignments. Sometimes parents get the impression that teachers disrespect students' native tongues or linguistic variations—even students' multilinguistic competence. Who says that Standard English is more academic, more worthy of being taught? Invite your students to ask adults they know about the experiences they have had with language. Often these stories substantiate your claims better than anything else. Consider reading and talking about the poem "The Phone Booth at the Corner" by Juan Delgado, which relates such a situation. Since few students are familiar with phone booths, you may need to show them a picture of how one works.

Why speak Standard English? That is a good question. Consider what you experienced in your own college or postcollege education training. Recall your exposure to the scholarly lingo, the "educationese." The American aphorist Mason Cooley once said, "An academic dialect is perfected when its terms are hard to understand and refer only to one another."[2] That is what some parents and students think about what is being taught in the schools. The language can seem like "school lingo," especially when it comes to the study and use of grammar. But it should not be limited to in-school speaking and writing.

Proficiency in speaking and writing Standard English is the ticket to career advancement in many professions. For this reason educators have the responsibility to help students acquire this language even while honoring students' heart or heritage languages, the language with which they are most comfortable and consider their own. By so doing effective teachers model what it means to respect others' languages and cultures.

In the ancient world, this was the basis for hospitality—making room for the "stranger" who is different from us and our culture. You can teach and honor by respecting the students' ability to communicate effectively in their own codes. When you do this, you may realize that you also are a stranger. Why? Because one's standard grammar and mother tongue are different than the linguistic norms of others. By practicing linguistic hospitality, students and teachers learn what it is like for others to be strangers, and all come to recognize one's own "strangeness."

Honor students' home language as you teach Standard English

THE VALUE OF STANDARD ENGLISH: A PERSONAL STORY

The occasion to demonstrate the value of speaking Standard English occurred when a friend invited me to present in classes at the Youth Tutoring Youth Program in Rochester, New York. This community project offered high school students an opportunity to learn the skills necessary to tutor elementary and middle school students in after-school programs. During the week prior to my visit, my friend Nettie sang my praises. She told students that I was an experienced teacher who had also had a successful sales career. Student expectations were high.

When I arrived, dressed rather casually, I quietly sidled into the classroom without saying a word until I was introduced. Then I began speaking in slang, using the street English vernacular similar to the dialect of that community. The students looked at each other askance, puzzled that my preestablished ethos (thanks to my friend!) did not match the image I conveyed in my attire, posture, and speech. As part of my monologue, I fumbled with my papers and blurted, "Oh darn it! I can't find my notes." I fled the room as if to retrieve them from somewhere out in the hall.

The students erupted with comments to each other and with questions to my friend. "She don't sound like a teacher, do she?" "I thought you said this woman is educated!" "She don't look like it!" "Where'd you get her from?" "Teachers ain't supposed to sound like that!"

My friend let them talk for a few minutes. I stood outside the classroom door, quickly removed the vest that clashed with my blouse, straightened my skirt, and with briefcase and notes in hand reentered the room. This time, I walked more erectly to the front of the room, addressed the class in Standard English, and then invited them to repeat their impressions of when they had first seen and heard me.

When asked why they were surprised, and even disappointed, in my appearance and speech, the students acknowledged the disconnection between their preconceptions and my presentation. They eventually admitted that, based on their teacher's description of my educational background and experience, they had expected me to speak "better" English. They realized and soon grasped the fact that just as they had made assumptions about me based on my clothing, grammar, and articulation, others could make the same assumptions about them. Point made.

The form of English that one knows and uses is important. The way one speaks and writes Standard English makes a difference in the way one is perceived by others. These students had witnessed firsthand the practical value of code-switching and were ready and open to practicing another way of speaking. Lesson learned.

LET AUTHORS MODEL FOR YOU

Showing your students ways that published authors use dialect to create valid and interesting stories is another reason to conclude a short fiction unit asking students to write their own stories. When they focus on their own writing while also thinking about others' prose, your normally impatient students become more conscientious about revising their own work. They realize that they have to think about their characters and readers, and especially about communicating with the reader as authentically and respectfully as possible. These young writers then realize they must get it right on behalf of the people they are writing about, not just for themselves.

Some students, inspired by fiction, decide to incorporate dialect or syntax that reflects the oral language of a specific ethnic group or geographical region. If other authors can do it, students reason, why can't they? Why shouldn't they at least try? If it is appropriate for their story, by all means give them the freedom to try it. But your aspiring writers need to know that it is easy to offend those for whom a dialect is their own. The easiest place to start is writing within one's own dialect. Even then, here is the key: students need to understand that when they write in their own voice—the voice of the

Urge, but do not insist, students to use Standard English in class

linguistic group with which they identify—they are making a choice with consequences for them as well as their readers.

Fortunately, many students are already learning some code-switching by writing for digital media. They learn "texting" on a cell phone or tweeting online. They learn that writing blogs is somewhat similar to journaling. Some write "fan fiction" on popular websites, trying to imitate their favorite writers. In other words, school students tend to be published code-switchers already even if they do not think of Facebook, SnapChat, Twitter, or other social networking websites as "publications" with their own styles and rules. Moreover, whether they like it or not, students realize others are interpreting and evaluating what and how they write.

CONCLUSION

Language arts are about life and the human condition. Professionals, like you, are called on to teach many grammars of code-switching and code-blending, using words and images in text, audio and verbal, print and digital media. The job is not to promote particular cultures or languages over others but to make sure that students are competent in Standard English and develop the basic ability to move from nonstandard idiolect to standard and back, or learning to blend the two when appropriate.

You are called on to show the appreciation of your students' languages as well as the particular language arts skills you bring. You do this because you recognize that knowing and understanding language is practical; language is an art as well as a skill, a means for all human beings to be able to understand and be understood, to serve others and be served by them. Language essentially is at the center of who we are as people, cultures, nations, ethnic groups, communities, religious groups, and the like.

Studying language as it is written and spoken helps students to understand communication and to practice it more ethically and effectively. You see, it is primarily through visual and verbal language that your students begin to understand what separates people and what unifies them. Honoring linguistic abilities, then, is a major component of honoring those shared differences. Through the lessons you design, you show your students that all humans share this amazing ability to switch codes in the midst of the very differences that confuse and divide people.

As an educator you can model respect, thus teaching your students to honor differences. And when students question why a "great" author can break the rules while a student might be viewed as inept, or is marked down for using the same nonstandard code, the answer is straightforward: students need to be able to switch from one to another linguistic variation depending on the setting. Most school writing is the setting for using Standard English.

NOTES

1. Heather Hansen, "Speak English Clearly and Grammatically, and Boost your Success!" Articles Base, n.d., http://leadershiptrainingtutorials.com/leadership-training/uncategorized/speak-english-clearly-and-grammatically-andboost-your-success/#.W4AnyOhKhAE (accessed November 12, 2018).
2. "Mason Cooley," *Brainy Quotes*, n.d. http://www.brainyquote.com/quotes/quotes/m/masoncoole396165.html (accessed November 12, 2018).

Chapter 4

Think on Paper: Writing in the Content Areas

> Writing in math gives me a window into my students' thoughts that I don't normally get when they just compute problems. It shows me their roadblocks, and it also gives me, as a teacher, a road map.
>
> —Maggie Johnson[1]

Writing is a means of expressing, exploring, and expanding our understanding. Those who teach in content areas other than English can tap into this powerful neurological experience to enhance the learning of the teacher about the students and the students about their subject. According to research conducted during my pursuit of a Master of Arts degree, I learned how important it is to have students write about their experiences learning and that if they are not writing in their own words in less than a month, students often experience retention loss of more than three-quarters of what they are taught.

This amazing research compels teachers in all content areas to consider ways to incorporate a range of writing opportunities in their lessons. As you mull over whether this practice is worthwhile, know that writing in and of itself is a heuristic, a way of knowing. As students search for words to express themselves, they are thinking about what they know and are able to do.

To be beneficial, writing for this purpose does not have to be collected, read, or graded. It can be used as preparation for talking about newly taught concepts and reflecting on ones being practiced. On the other hand, on quizzes and tests, when teachers include questions requiring students to explain how to solve problems, writing can be graded for clarity and accuracy. This works in math, science, social studies, art, music, and other courses, as well as English classes.

The benefit of assigning writing to learn is two fold: expressive/exploratory writing activities increase the confidence and competence of students taking the course. This kind of writing also provides an ongoing evaluation tool for assessing what students are learning without giving stressful tests or dealing with tedious grading assignments. The second value of adding writing to learn to your instructional practices is bringing your teaching in line with current curricula goals in your content area standards.

Teachers soon see how writing can show how students understand various processes in solving problems in math, science, and social studies. For longer-term retention of information, it is important that students write regularly, not just for semester-long research assignments, reflection, and revision but also every few days just to self-assess and confirm learning.[2]

Reading what students write helps teachers diagnose more quickly specific deficiencies and measure understanding of various content-specific concepts and their applications. This kind of writing stimulates metacognition and verbalization—both talking and writing—and encourages shared inquiry

All student writing need not be graded

when you invite students to discuss and question their peers in collaborative/cooperative learning group activities.

SHOWING WRITING IS REVEALING

When and where should students do this kind of writing? Several times a week in their paper or digital journals. In addition to their traditional class notes, students can:

- record specific concepts they believe they learned after an in-class presentation or homework assignment;
- react to what they are learning or what they are assigned but not learning;
- explain how to perform specific procedures in math, science, art, or gym; and
- explain how to read graphs, charts, and maps in history/social science.

Students in Emily Espy's eighth-grade math class demonstrate the benefits of explanatory writing in tasks designed to build students' verbal reasoning and problem-solving skills. Her students write their reasons for decisions made based on math computations. For example, a practical task found in illustrative mathematics asks students to determine which flower vase would be best for a customer who wants a container to hold enough water to keep her flowers fresh while she was away from home several days.

Ms. Espy's students had to figure the volume of each sample vase, show their work, recommend a vase, and explain their answer. Most curricula ask teachers to assess student learning formatively and summatively. This kind of writing can help validate what students know and are able to do throughout the course.

What do these kinds of assignments look like? The student samples are from my booklet "Writing to Learn in Math: Collaboration/Cooperation—Learning Pairs and Groups,"[3] written for teachers interested in implementing this kind of writing to learn.

EXPRESSING, EXPLORING, DISCOVERING

Expressive writing is the kind of writing students do that puts into words what they think they are learning. This writing is very much like speech. It usually is uncensored for grammatical correctness and intended to communicate with the writer, not with the teacher/reader. The students put into their own words their understanding of what is going on in the math or science problem and how they feel about what they are learning.

> 10/28
> Dear Journal:
> My first C!! Boy did I bomb this baby! My mistakes are mostly careless and since I didn't get time to check it, they couldn't be corrected. Some of the word problems were misinterrupted [sic] and so my answers weren't checked out. The exponent mistakes were just stupid!
>
> —EM

Exploratory writing is the kind of writing students do that helps them figure out how to solve certain procedures. Exploratory writing can be assigned in science, math, or history/social sciences classes to have students show they know the correct way to cite resources in the school-required format. So much better to discover this early, before that ream of research papers comes in for grading.

> 9/28
> $3(x5) = 1/5(10x25)$ You should distribute 3 and 1/5 to the numbers. Then you would get the ex's to the left and the 3's to the right. Then you should simplify and solve. Ones I can't do are $c-2y=b$. I cannot understand this! Which variable do you solve? How could you do it? I don't UNDERSTAND!!!! I was trying to solve for Yb instead of just solving. I missed what the book said.
>
> —JL

Discovery writing is the kind of writing students do when they analyze and figure what they know about the various assignments they are given. In assignments that call for this kind of writing, students look carefully at the kind of errors they made on specific assignments and then write what they discovered about their own work.

> 10/28
> Dear Journal:
> I could of done better on the test. I got two wrong on the exponents which I knew how to do but forgot. I made one silly error on Sci. Not (Scientific Notation) by forgetting it was a negative (insert 10 (–4 exponent). One part I did not know the difference between of % and more than % and on the chemical prop I set it up right but worked it out wrong. And I messed up on the age problems. Now I know to stick with the first answer.
>
> —BA

You probably notice that the student entries include elements of multiple kinds of writing: expressive, exploratory, and discovery. This will be true of the writing to learn your students do, too. To be most useful, assign this kind of writing early in the course, and continue doing so on a regular basis. Part of the value of expressive/exploratory/discovery writing is the fluency that develops once students are used to it. They begin to look forward to the opportunity to unravel their thoughts and be prepared to ask focused questions of clarification of you and of their peers.

CLARIFYING TEACHING AND FOCUSING STUDY

Consider adapting ideas from this series of activities to maximize your students' learning experience. Your writing test questions that require students to explain how they solve problems can elicit strong evidence of their understanding in ways that showing work in numbers only cannot reveal. You and your students begin approaching learning in more positive ways when writing regularly is part of the course. You find yourself preparing with more care and clarity as you think about what you will ask students to know well enough to write at the beginning, middle, and end of the unit.

Students respond to these writing-to-learn assignments by paying attention to their textbook reading and in-class activities because they know they will be asked to articulate their understanding in their own words. Students begin to:

- focus on their assignments and performance;
- analyze reasons for the success or failure in the subject;
- reflect on what they read in their text and experience in class;
- verbalize more comfortably in written and oral forms with you and their classmates; and
- collaborate more confidently because they already have begun thinking and finding words to express themselves more precisely.

Of course, none of these is isolated. A student may focus and analyze during a reflection and verbalize during a collaborative situation. Your goal is to understand and design writing and speaking assignments that enhance the teaching and learning experiences in your classroom.

Kiondre Dunham, a history teacher in a middle school, finds having his students write summaries and reflections serves as a formative assessment for both him and his students. He can see whether or not students are ready to move on to the next concept. Furthermore, when students see they can express their thoughts in this informal way, they can know for themselves that they are learning. This, of course, increases their confidence and helps them remain open to further instruction.

TALKING TEACHES

Combining writing activities with talking in collaborative pairs, triads, and small group discussions enriches the learning experience. Once students have written their thoughts about what they are learning or not learning, they have words to talk about it with peer partners and in whole class discussion. As you circulate among the pairs—observing, listening, and peeking over their shoulders at what the students have written—you can quickly determine what students know or still find confusing and adjust the lesson to meet the current state of their learning, comfort or discomfort.

Add Paired Sharing

You can vary the kind of writing you assign based on the lessons you are teaching. For example, if students have had what you know has been a challenging homework assignment, you may begin the next class assigning an "admit slip" on which students write a sentence or two admitting and acknowledging what proved difficult for them to understand. Ask them to be specific and refer to the section or page of the handout or text. Then ask students to pull their desks or chairs together so they can work in pairs, using their six-inch voices to discuss the question/problem and try to come up with a response using class notes or their textbooks.

Pairing students can maximize in-class instruction time

Another time, while presenting a particularly complex lesson, stop and ask students to write a summary. For this, they can write three or four sentences in their own words about what they are hearing, such as:

- a definition of a concept;
- a summary of what they have learned so far; or
- a question they have about what has been presented or viewed.

Allow a couple of minutes for a few students to read aloud what they have written. These readings can reinforce the value of writing while revealing whether or not the students are grasping the ideas being presented. Frequently students will phrase the definition in words more familiar to their classmates and more easily comprehensible than those in the formal definition, academic or content-specific vocabulary you may have used.

In another setting, it may be valuable to have students practice answering questions themselves. Collect the slips and redistribute them to students on the opposite side of the class. Give the students a minute or two to read the slips to see if they can resolve the issue themselves. It may take a few times of working this way for students to stay focused on task. If they get off task, immediately stop the session and have students return desks and chairs to the regular format.

Resist the temptation to berate the students for getting off task. It may take a couple of weeks for them to be comfortable with this kind of vulnerability. As you cultivate trust in them and model courteous commenting, the students soon follow your lead. When they get off task, gently call attention to the front and go on with the lesson of the day, using the admit or summary slips to guide your instruction for the remainder of the period.

The next day, allot just a little less time for paired talking; then on subsequent days, extend the time in half-minute increments until you reach five to six minutes. Circulating among the pairs helps maintain order and provides opportunities to listen, observe, and redirect attention as necessary. Students will come to value this time to figure out answers and clarify their thinking.

The exit slip can be used in similar way. Five minutes before the end of the period, distribute 3 × 5 cards or pieces of scrap paper to each student. If they are working on computers, have them send you a message on one of those apps. Ask students to write in their own words what you taught that period and what they have learned. Again, content, not form, is important in these notes. Merely collect these anonymous notes as students leave the classroom. Reading them later will give a better idea of what concepts the students have grasped and which need further clarification before proceeding on to new material.

Reading what they write reveals how they are thinking

All three—the admit, summary, and exit slips—are effective ways for both student and teacher to learn. If the students can find the words to write fairly clearly what was they know, they know they know; if they can't, they know too that and can either ask for help or study themselves. They do not have to wait until a graded assignment to learn what they know. This kind of writing helps tell who knows what, now.

ANALYZING MAY BE
UNCOMFORTABLE BUT VALUABLE WRITING

After a particularly challenging unit, you could ask students to analyze that experience by responding to such prompts as the following:

- What problem or kind of problem was most difficult for you—one that you are proud you could answer?
- What problem or kind of problem could you not solve?
- Try to describe the errors or kind of errors you made most.

Another math teacher, Cassidy Earle, has her sixth-grade students write after a summative assessment. They respond to prompts that ask how they felt about their grade and how they prepared for the test. One student wrote,

> *The test was normal. Scary. The thought of your grade is scary and it messes you up. If you study you are ready and if you don't rest in peace. I used my notes and my journal. . . . My parents were working, so I had to study alone. . . . I am good with numbers, but not so much in geometry, so I might need to try harder.*

The purpose of this informal writing assignment is to gain insight into students' thinking about math, not to measure the accuracy of their grammar, spelling, punctuation, and sentence structure. If you understand what they are saying, there is no need to use red pen to circle or deduct credit for such minor errors.

Through the post-assessment reflections, teachers gain insight into students who have test anxiety, those who may be home alone regularly, those who had little time to study for math because they had three other tests the same day, and those whose English comprehension skills may make it difficult for some to comprehend the story problems and test prompts. Such specific details can help address issues with students and those raised by parents, administrators, and colleagues in other courses.

WRITING THE STEPS

This comforting activity is a version of the summary sentence and can work well in a math, science, physical education, music, or ceramics art class. After explaining a new procedure for an important process in your class, have students write in order, in their own words, the steps to completing that task. It could be solving a math problem, setting up a lab, calling a foul, tuning an instrument, or preparing a piece of clay before throwing on the wheel.

Ask the students to turn and talk to a partner or group about the steps they wrote. As the steps are read, all can listen to these versions and can hear various ways of stating the procedure. When necessary take time to clarify any cloudiness or confusion. Resist the temptation to force students to use formal language if what they have written is correct.

Somehow, this can be a reassuring exercise for the class. All can hear how classmates are thinking/not thinking and recognize that they are not alone in getting/not getting the new material. At the same time, you can monitor and adjust as needed. By writing the steps, the students can focus and reflect, figure out, and clarify their thinking under your guidance, thus advancing the learning for more students in less time.

Writing about learning deepens it

REFLECTING ON TEST PERFORMANCE

It takes some students years to learn how to take tests and how to learn from the kinds of mistakes they make, so allot a full-class meeting to go over tests when you return them. What kind of topics should you cover during test analysis? First, ask students to determine the kinds of errors they made. Did they make errors because of the following reasons:

- misreading the question or prompt;
- running out of time;
- misunderstanding a concept, term, or instruction;
- studying the wrong material;
- failing to respond to the question;
- missing clues to answers in the prompt or stem of multiple choice question; or
- some other reason.

Once students determine the kinds of errors they made, talk about ways to avoid them next time. Usually students calm down when they learn that correcting one problem before the next test can help them lose fewer points the next time. See textbox 4.1 for question prompts to use at the end of the term.

> **TEXTBOX 4.1 POST-EXAM ANALYSIS**
>
> 1. I am pleased that _____
> 2. I am surprised/disappointed that _____
> 3. My score is lower because of (mark appropriate reasons)_____
> 4. _____ misread instructions _____ careless errors inaccurate _____ not enough details
> 5. _____ incomplete answers _____ wrong material studied _____ other (explain)
> 6. To prepare for this exam, I _____
> 7. This exam accurately/inaccurately reflects what we learned this semester. (Please explain.) _____
> 8. Qtr 1 _____ × 37.5% + Qtr 2 _____ × 37.5% + Exam _____ × 25% = Semester Grade _____
> 9. Based on this analysis, I see my strengths are _____
> 10. This next semester, I must focus on _____
>
> _____   _____
> Student Signature   Parent/Guardian Signature

CONCLUSION

Combining writing-to-learn activities with collaborative talking is an efficient way to use class time. Once students have written responses in their journals and turned and talked with their partners, they often can resolve problems on their own. This concurrent learning is less time consuming than your answering all their questions one by one. However, periodically collecting this kind of writing can be vital to your understanding of students and planning future lessons that target their needs while meeting your course goals.

As you circulate among them, listening and observing, you learn right away what needs more instruction and time for practice or what is clearly understood and therefore can be tested with confidence. Writing as part of periodic test analyses generally improves test performance.

Therefore, if you are among those who are reluctant to add writing to learn in classroom practices, you can relax. Unless the question is part of a test, this is ungraded writing. It is designed for you and your students to process what is taught and being learned. Reading what students write provides a window into their understanding which, as a no-stress formative assessment, effectively guides you in future lesson planning. Being asked to write helps students know what they know and how to zone in on what they do not know—yet.

NOTES

1. Vicki Urquhart, "Using Writing in Math to Deepen Student Learning" (Mid-continent Research for Education and Learning). 2009. https://files.eric.ed.gov/fulltext/ED544239.pdf (accessed February 25, 2018).
2. "Standards for Math Practice." *Common Core State Standards Implementation.* 2012. http://www.corestandards.org/Math/Content/8/introduction (accessed June 23, 2018).
3. Anna J. Small Roseboro, "Writing and Learning Groups in Math" (unpublished master's thesis for University of California, San Diego), 1989.

Chapter 5

Tell It Like It Is: Inviting Informative Writing

> People are usually more convinced by reasons they discovered themselves than by those found out by others.
>
> —Blaise Pascal[1]

Writing is a personal way to express oneself. While purpose determines the mode one uses, arrangement, length, style, and vocabulary remain the choice of the author. This fact creates a dilemma for teachers who are charged to teach their students specific ways to write and may be obligated to test them on their ability to write in several different modes. Without careful planning, this predicament may reduce the time allotted for students to choose the most effective ways of communicating to achieve their own goals. This chapter describes ways to manage this quandary with suggestions for teaching the basics and then freeing students to write for personal purposes.

In the classroom, it sometimes is easy to lose sight of the ultimate goal of education—to help students acquire knowledge and develop the range of skills needed to live self-sufficient, productive lives in a pluralistic society. However, as teachers work backward, accepting that goal and planning lessons to help reach it, they learn to stay on track without becoming rigidly shortsighted.

Therefore, what does this have to do with teaching students how to write? It means remembering that our classroom is a training ground where we, like athletic coaches, introduce new information, demonstrate skills, and then schedule opportunities for students to practice writing. But finally, when the game begins, we trust our burgeoning writers to choose what works in the heat of the game—when they want to express themselves in writing.

Standards like those used in your course generally require teachers to present a range of strategies for prewriting, revision, editing, and publishing that have proven to be effective for different kinds of writing and purposes. Successful educators somehow learn to do this without insisting that every student execute each step in the same way for every assignment. You know from your own schooling, college training, and work in the classroom that there probably are as many different configurations for prewriting, drafting, and revising as are years you have been on this earth! None works well for every writer every time. Ask the zillion published authors out there.

Therefore, how does one teach in light of this reality? Make plans guided by the curriculum standards and remain flexible. Ideas here can help you plot a course for this part of your school year voyage. No need to worry. You can navigate the tricky waters without fearing Scylla and Charybdis, those rocks and whirlpools that could distract you from teaching writing effectively.

LEARNING FROM A STUDENT: A PERSONAL STORY

After weeks of instruction, I just knew my young writers were ready to move on to the next step: Applying what they'd learned about the writing process in an on-demand timed setting. *I'd taught them well. They'd responded enthusiastically. Now, I thought, is their time to shine and my time to gloat! Not.*

They arrive to see an engaging prompt on the board and the start and stop times written prominently as a reminder to pace themselves. Now, to commence the show. Students pull out pens, sheets of lined paper, and a piece of scratch paper on which to create their pre-writes. No more questions? They get started.

I stroll around the room, observing their writing and nodding as I notice that nearly every option for prewriting appears among the papers I can see. Good!

Then, I spot one girl across the room gazing off into space. "Hmmm. Why isn't she writing?" Carefully, so as not to alarm anyone, I quickly make my way over to her desk and peer around her shoulder. I glower in disbelief. Her paper is blank, nothing there, no list, no diagram, no drawing; nothing after nearly fifteen minutes into the period! How is she going to finish in time?

I lean down and whisper, "What's the holdup? When are you going to get started?"

The girl whispers back, "I'm thinking."

A little louder, but still keeping my voice low, I point and ask, "Can't you see the clock?"

"Yeah, I see it. I'm OK. I'm thinking."

"When are you going to start writing?"

"When I can see my paper."

"See your paper?" I quietly yell. She scowls, letting me know she has things under control and won't I just trust her and shut up and let her finish, for crying out loud; don't I see the clock?

I get the message, shrug my shoulders, purse my lips, and let it go, dooming her to her fate. She is going to be a disappointment. I certainly don't look forward to reading a paper not written the way I'd spent all this time teaching.

As you probably surmised, this student's paper was one of the better ones in the bunch. I was surprised, yes, and just a little disenchanted. I apparently hadn't been the one to teach her how to write so well in a timed setting. Who had?

Afterward, wanting to understand, I invited the student in to talk about the paper. I asked how she organized her thoughts if she wasn't using any of the prewriting strategies I'd demonstrated so assiduously and seen her practice so enthusiastically. The young lady didn't appear the least bit reticent and freely acknowledged that she'd done all the exercises because they were fun, but they didn't really work that well for her. Is that so!

The student explained to me that she produced better writing when she brainstormed, organized, and reorganized her thoughts in her head. She even visualized what her paper would look like. Then she just wrote what she saw.

"Well! That's just great," I thought. "How am I going to grade a student's pre-write if I can't see it. Should I insist she do things the way I taught her, just so I'd have something to grade? Even if what she produces is good without them?" Thanks a lot for this quandary!

The young lady left. I sat trying to sort out my thoughts. Then I recalled some of the research about multiple intelligences and the need for differentiating instruction. Students process information in different ways. Here is concrete evidence. While this student does not fall into the typical alternative categories that show up on the charts (auditory, kinesthetic, musical, etc.), hers definitely is a different style from those I have encountered before. I'll have to make some adjustments. What I learned from experience and reading apparently is not all there is to writing.

After that incident, I recognized the need for even more flexibility and differentiation in my teaching and in the options I offer for students to show what they know. More of my assignments began to include student choice within teacher controls—guided, but not constrained, by curriculum demands and grade-level standards. I conscientiously focused on what I have to assess while planning lessons and, then during instruction, strived to articulate for the students what I needed to measure about their learning to confirm their level of understanding and degree of skill development. No—this is not the same as "teaching to the test." Instead, it simply means offering alternative

Students resort to strategies that work for them

assessments and letting students choose ways they can best show what they know. I urge you to do the same.

WRITING RIGHT: JUST THE RIGHT MODE FOR THE OCCASION

The five-paragraph essay is one of many structures you may be expected to teach. It is a formula designed to encourage students to flesh out their writing by developing their position statements into meaty paragraphs. However, this prescribed mold does not work well for some students, and it is seldom seen in professional publications. Therefore, rather than adhere strictly to a formula that can stifle writing, teach it as an option but do not require that every student write this way for every essay assigned. Ask your students to try each structure, and then let them choose which works better for them.

Alternatively, teach students the parts of an essay—introduction, body, and conclusion—as well as the function, purpose, or responsibility of each of these parts. For some students, writing three paragraphs is sufficient for what they have to say and the way they can say it best. For others, four will suffice; other may need six or more paragraphs. In other words, be flexible about the number of paragraphs students are permitted to write. Instead, insist that the final essay include the necessary parts.

ACTING OUT AN ESSAY

How about a little kinesthetic activity to help students understand the structure of an essay? You could invite small groups of seven to ten students to demonstrate an essay that has the three requisite parts. Jock Mackenzie, author of *Essay Writing: Teaching the Basics from the Ground Up*, recommends instructing students to organize themselves into an essay with at least three groups—to represent the introduction, the body, and the conclusion.[2] This may take a little time, so help pace the steps using your timer.

For the first step, set your timer for five to seven minutes, depending on the number of students and the classroom space. Then step aside, listen, and watch how students decide who should stand where and why. When the buzzer rings, ask students to freeze and look around.

You could ask those in the introduction section to raise their hands; those in the section(s) for body paragraph(s) to raise their hands, and then those in the conclusion section to do the same.

What are you looking to see? Proportion. Are there fewer students in the introduction and conclusion sections? Next, direct the subgroups to move into separate corners of the room. Each group—introduction, body, and conclusion—is to come up with a gesture or body pose to indicate the function of their part of the essay. Again, set the timer for five to seven minutes; step aside, observe, and listen to what they do and say. What may you see?

The introduction group may arrange themselves into a triangle, with each member gesturing forward with his or her pointer finger to indicate the introduction shows the way the essay will go. One person may represent the thesis statement. The body group may arrange themselves into two or more smaller groups to indicate multiple paragraphs. Each subgroup may have one student representing the topic sentence. The conclusion group may stand and gesture "time-out" to indicate the essay is coming to an end. This group may arrange itself in a triangle and point thumbs over shoulders to indicate the conclusion may look back to point to what has already been developed in the body.

Finally, ask the students to demonstrate the need for transitions between sections and between sentences by reaching out and linking pinky fingers. Yes, they will giggle, but that's typical. Then, call a freeze, a pause for silence. If you have a digital camera or cell phone, snap a photo before directing students to return to their seats.

Close with a debriefing session reflecting on the choices they made and how their final tableau did, in fact, demonstrate the structure of an essay. In the lessons to come, remind them of this exercise and maybe point to the photo of them that you post on the bulletin board or upload into a slide you can project during class.

CHOOSING TOPICS FOR WRITING

An effective way to get to know the travelers on a trip through the school year is to invite them to talk about themselves. This also is an efficient way to obtain baseline writing samples. Talking and writing about themselves removes the additional burden of showing what they know about an assigned topic, a piece of fiction or nonfiction writing they have read. Your student writers can pay attention to organization, sentence structure, and choice of language. You can wait until later in the year to see how well they can pull evidence from literary or informational texts to support analysis, reflection, and research as set forth in many curriculum standards for English language arts.[3]

Yes, some students are reluctant to write about personal matters in an unfamiliar classroom or uncomfortable setting. It may take weeks before the environment of your classroom feels safe. Therefore, design assignments with the option to fictionalize details. One such assignment asks students to think about their futures, the value of education, and career planning. It is a human-interest story—about themselves or someone they know. While you know that the choices they make still will be revealing, the students experience the detachment that makes them feel more secure.

Consider the following human-interest story. It combines the two—opportunity to talk about themselves and to fictionalize a future event. It even has an option for conducting informal research as students consider the qualifications for certain awards. As they do, students discover awards are given for outstanding performance, contributions and/or excellence in a career: community service, philanthropy, science, the arts, sports, and other areas. Your students may consider well-known Nobel Prize awards in the various categories; the Oscars, Grammy, Tony, and other awards for the arts; Halls of Fame for various sports: Cy Young Award, MVP awards; rodeo, fishing, ballroom dancing; Miss America or Mr. Universe, or those lesser known but coveted awards given in your hometown or state.

With minor editing, these articles will make fine additions to your class bulletin board, class website, or something to send home in letters to families.

HUMAN-INTEREST STORY

With what prestigious award will you be honored in twenty-five years?

Paragraph 1
Who, what, when, where, why, and how about award ceremony

Paragraph 2
Education and career of winner (you in twenty-five years)

Paragraph 3
Others who have won the honor in the past

Paragraph 4
Ways this year's winner (you) compares to former winners

Paragraph 5
When and where award will be given next year

After revising and editing your article, add a recent photo of yourself.

DISCOVERING PURPOSES
AND ORGANIZATION PATTERNS

You have required curriculum to follow, right? As general policy, introducing or reviewing specific modes of writing, letting students write about themselves, and giving students choices all sound good, but you still may not be sure where to start. Why not at the beginning with a couple of exploratory adventures based on the texts students will encounter in your course?

Plan a lesson for students to discover or review the elements in the different modes. Begin brainstorming, asking students to think about reasons people would want to write in the first place. The list should include the following purposes:

- to inform
- to explain
- to report
- to argue
- to persuade
- to entertain

Use the students' words at first to validate their contribution. You then can move along in a later lesson, to use the more formal terms they may see later. It will be important for them to know the academic vocabulary to be successful in other educational settings, like those standardized or end-of-the-year exams many schools administer.

SETTING UP THE DISCOVERY EXPEDITION

Gather age-appropriate samples or mentor texts of different types of writing. Look in your textbook and online for writing on topics that interest your students or that introduce topics you plan to teach later in the school year. No need to leave out humorous essays. They sometimes are more accessible and memorable.

Resist the temptation to rush the process by giving students clues ahead of time. Let them discover by talking with partners or in small groups. Create slides with the step-by-step instructions so those who may not be paying attention can glance up, confirm they heard you right, and get back to work. Usually one slide per step will suffice. Advance the slides as the class completes each step. Have your timer ready set for three or four minutes depending on length or writing and skill of your student readers.

- Hand out colored pencils and ask students to read silently the sample and mark anything they notice that may be a clue to the kind of essay they have.
- Exchange pencils for a new color. Read the sample again, this time marking what they recognize in terms of text structure and organization.

- Exchange pencils once more, getting a third color. This time, read and mark in the left margin symbols to indicate the beginning, middle, and end of one of the essays. Students may need four to five minutes for this task.
  - a triangle pointing down next to the beginning section
  - a rectangle where the middle or body begins
  - a triangle pointing up to mark the start of the ending section
- Finally, ask students to write what they think is the purpose of their sample essay: to inform, explain, compare, argue, persuade, entertain, or whatever.

During this initial ten to twelve minutes that students are working independently, remember to circulate among them paying attention to which students get right to work. Who seems to be puzzled and needs you to re-explain what they should be doing? Your physical proximity helps these young investigators stay focused and to ask questions without attracting the embarrassing attention of their peers. Remember to advance your slides showing what students should be doing for each reading. As time allows, write some anecdotal notes about what you observe regarding specific students and the class as a whole.

STUDENTS MAY POINT OUT MULTIPLE FEATURES

- Be prepared for students to notice that essays often reflect multiple structures. Few pieces of writing reflect a single structure. Writers sometimes use narratives, tell stories, as they attempt to persuade their readers. Some writers write descriptive passages when their goal is simply to report.
- Invite student speakers to explain to the others how they labeled their sample(s) and what organization and text-structure clues helped them decide the purpose of their sample essay. As before, listen and observe to help decide what they already know and what still needs clarification. Thankfully, students often are good teachers and save valuable time by explaining the key points in ways their peers understand.
- Finally, call the class together to merge their findings and to reflect on what they have discovered. How consistent are the findings? What characteristics do students notice in different samples?

Another day, you may project two or three sample essays and invite students to come forward and point to different parts, signal words, and other characteristics of the essay. Encourage them to use the academic language as much as possible.

Teaching is more than telling

TAKING TIME FOR DISCOVERY

These discovery expeditions may take two or three days. No need to rush. If it makes sense to send the samples home for homework review, do so. Then during the next class meeting, reassemble the adventurers at the start of class. If this kind of homework is unrealistic, begin the next class meeting in groups to review what they discovered. After the independent and whole class experience with samples, the students are likely to have detected some of the patterns of organizing that you taught them to watch for when they are reading to learn:

- description
- sequential order
- problem/solution
- compare/contrast
- cause/effect
- directions
- narrative, telling a story

You can try to keep it simple at first, but be prepared for students to notice that a writer may use one or more of these structures to fulfill any of the purposes for writing: to inform, to argue, to persuade, or to entertain. Therefore, you really are asking students to try to identify the purpose for the writing, to notice the use of text structures as well as the patterns of organization.

It is also likely that your discerning students may find it difficult to distinguish between the samples you may have included that illustrate argument and those that exemplify persuasion. You may have to point out, after such a comment, that argumentation simply presents opposing views and maybe adds reasons for believing one side or the other, while persuasion usually has a call for action or a plea to change one's belief or behavior.

TEACHING IS MORE THAN TELLING

Yes, this kind of teaching will take more time than your giving a simple lecture, showing a set of slides with definitions, or even labeling the writing samples and highlighting the different features for them; in that case, *you* will have done the thinking. More effective teaching and long-term retention occur when students seek out and find answers for themselves. You may use alternative methods of lesson delivery until the majority of students can demonstrate they have learned. Effective teachers teach spirally, drawing earlier lessons into current ones so students hear, see, and do enough to develop proficiency. In the long run, this could mean less reteaching on your part or that of next year's teachers. What students discover for themselves, they remember.

Even with increased implementation of teaching strategies that appeal to the multiple intelligences, consider building in reteaching but with a twist. Plan multisensory lessons that require students to use physical as well as mental muscles like the earlier activity that asked for students to "act out an essay." Design lessons that have something for students to see, to hear, and to do. Note recommendations for each of these kinds of presentations as you continue reading this book.

Will you have to remind students of what they have seen, heard, and done? Of course. You very well may have some of these same students in later grades and shake your head that they will have forgotten so much of what you thought you had taught so well.

That probably is the main reason students have English classes the majority of the years they are in school—not only because language arts form the basis for learning in most content areas but also because students forget or see no immediate use for what they are taught. If they do not use it, they lose it. Teachers, therefore, continue to provide multiple opportunities for students to exercise their skills so their thinking muscles do not atrophy, making it difficult to use these muscles when they need them. Allot time for students to write for real purposes.

Build a firm foundation but don't get stuck

BUILDING THE FOUNDATION FOR CONVINCING ARGUMENTATIVE ESSAYS

An effective road to teaching students to write argumentative essays is to take time to build on skills they already have learned. Most middle school students have been writing reports since third grade. It makes sense, then, to embark on this part of the trip that includes a direct writing instruction unit by having your students practice writing to inform. That simply requires students to gather, organize, and present facts in much the same way they wrote those elementary school science reports.

Therefore, begin there. "What," you could ask them, "are some of the reasons a person would want to write an informative essay?" Their answers are likely to include such things as to report, to explain, to describe, and to just share their feelings. You probably will have taught text structures already as they relate to reading; now is the time to have students demonstrate what they understand about text structures by employing those devices in their own writing. Post on your website, include on printed assignment, and display on your word wall some of the signal words—"because," "but," "for example," "however," "in conclusion"—used in published informative writing and that probably are listed in the texts you are using.

You could have students practice by reporting or explaining something they already know. Their topics could be drawn from literature, real life, or lessons students are learning in other content areas. Consider inviting your young companions on the road to use what they are learning in social studies and write about a historical event; explain how to accomplish a task—build something, cook, sail, fish, rope a steer, ride a horse, pop an "Ollie" on their skateboard, or strategize in a board or computer game. This is an excellent way to reinforce what your students are learning elsewhere, to validate the work of colleagues in other departments, and the value in English class for learning to write well.

To reduce student temptation to copy from published work, begin the drafting in class. If students then decide to do research before the final draft is due, remind them to cite their sources. As always on a multidraft assignment, students should date, keep, and turn in all drafts, earliest on the bottom and the latest on the top. If they are working online, save all drafts so they and you can see how their writing evolves. The varied topics students choose make for more interesting, even informative reading for you, too.

LOGICAL STEPS TO OTHER KINDS OF WRITING

The next logical step toward more complex writing would be to move on to the compare/contrast essays for which students gather, organize, and write about two different people, places, things, events, or ideas. To keep this concrete, again invite students to consider something they already know.

You could have them compare/contrast short stories they have read for your class and one they read on their own: a movie version versus print version; movies or television programs on the same topic; kinds of music; food; different computer games; clothes; animals; cars, bicycles, boats, fishing rods, or saddles, current event with one they read about in history or science. Let students choose.

Show your budding writers two basic ways of organizing compare/contrast essays, and invite them to use the pattern that works better for them. They could write the body of their paragraphs in blocks or stripes.

- Blocks
    - introduce the features to be considered
    - all comparisons or ways alike
    - all contrasts or ways different

- Stripes
    - feature of comparison 1—A and B together
    - feature of comparison 2—A and B together
    - feature of comparison 3—A and B together

Their task, of course, is to decide what features or elements to compare or contrast. A Venn diagram is an effective graphic organizer for brainstorming and arranging the facts and explanations about how the two subjects of the essay are alike or different or are both alike *and* different. For example, the students may look at two stories and compare the different ways the author employs literary devices: What point of view? Are there flashbacks? A dominant method of characterization? Use of realistic or stilted dialogue? Or keeping it personal, students may compare/contrast themselves and the main character in a biographical work they read.

For this basic compare/contrast essay, the students are simply reporting, but you may ask them to add an element of evaluation and state and explain which author the students think uses the elements more effectively; which product, song, or sport is better, or why fishing with one kind of rod is safer than another; which method is safer, more productive. Then the writers will be moving into argumentation, making a case for one story, product, behavior, or the other.

While it is okay to use "I think" and "I believe" in earlier drafts, ask the students to remove these phrases from the final draft. Just state their observations, and let those statements stand firmly on the reasons the student gives for taking those positions on the topic, thus encouraging students to develop confidence in their supported assertions.

CONNECTING WRITING TO CURRENT EVENTS

To keep the learning relevant, you could ask students to bring in samples from their reading that exemplify the kind of writing you are teaching. Several students come from homes where magazines and newspapers are regularly read. You can direct students to the school or neighborhood libraries where they can find samples in the magazines and newspapers to which most libraries subscribe. You could offer students minimum credit for bringing in articles, but no one should be penalized for not doing so. You know your school community and know to choose assignments that affirm the households from which your students come and resources that are readily available to them. Consider loaning them magazines from the stack you keep in your room.

If you know members of the class do not have comparable access to resources, consider scheduling a library visit or make this a triad or small group project. One student can bring in the article(s); another can mount them on white sheet(s) of paper and mark the parts; and another can speak for the group, describing the article(s)' contents, kind(s) of writing, and special features the group has noticed. Then plan a gallery walk for students to see and hear what their classmates have brought.

In a gallery walk, half of the groups sit facing one direction, with seats facing them. The other half of the group members would move from left to right and explain their sample to the group opposite them. Here is another situation where a timer is useful to keep the groups on track. In this activity, the value is in the students' talking and making decisions about how to present what they are learning about published writing. Your task is to listen and observe with a smile. You are learning and planning based on what you hear and see.

A benefit of assigning students to bring in samples is the insight you gain into what interests your students. You can use that knowledge to design subsequent assignments. Remind students to include the citation that includes the website name, title, authors, URL address, and date they access the article. Those who bring in printed articles should label them with source and date. Regularly remind them to be honorable young men and women who consistently give credit when they use the work of others.

It would be prudent to check all the articles brought in to assure they are appropriate for in-class discussion. These are, after all, students who may not yet know exactly what is off limits in the classroom. You can conduct an inspection subtly by having students bring in the article at least a day before you plan to use them in class. Just discretely remove questionable articles and offer that group a magazine from which to choose another. No need to create a scene. Some students have different sets of standards, and no matter how shocked you may be, you can help them develop discernment without embarrassing them.

What makes this kind of student-generated assignment so rich is that students tend to read more when they get to choose what to contribute. Students usually want to make sure they understand the selection just in case you ask them to talk about it! Some young students may want to impress you and their peers and bring in articles from *Business Week* or *Atlantic Monthly* that they or their parents regularly read. Then, too, even though your students may be middle schoolers, some truly may be interested in the articles in what generally are considered adult journals. Therefore, act as though you expected nothing less.

DECIDING HOW LONG

So far in these writing assignments, students are not being asked to argue a position to bring about a change in belief or behavior. They have been gathering facts and writing about them in some logically organized fashion. Whatever the assignments though, they probably have begun to ask "How long should this be?" You may be tempted to say, "Long enough to get the job done," which is a good answer but not very helpful to young or inexperienced writers. Instead, you could go on to tell them that to be complete, an essay, like a good story, should have at least three parts—a recognizable beginning, middle, and ending—and for an essay, the names of these parts are introduction, body, and conclusion.

Now would be a good time to review with your curious writers the function of each of these parts of an essay. Yes, even if you have bright, experienced ninth or tenth graders who have been writing very well all through middle school, you reinforce these functions in as much depth as needed with the students you currently are teaching and then hold them accountable

- for *introducing* their essays in ways that invite, intrigue, indicate direction, and guide the reader into the body of the essay;
- for *developing the middle* part of their essays with well-built paragraphs sequenced in a logical way; and
- for *concluding* their essays in a way that summarizes or reflects on what has been written (without repeating it), or projects onto the future considerations without introducing new information.

USING GRAPHICS TO SHOW STRUCTURE

Diagrams, cartoons, and other images can show the structure of an essay and function of each part. Using them enhances your instruction, making it easier for students to visualize different features of an effective essay. Consider the idea of a train. It is metaphor to illustrate both purpose and order that makes sense to students living in most geographical settings—city or country, mountain or plains. Show the engine, the cargo cars, and the caboose. They will get it.

Train couplings signify transitions

The engine is the introduction, gets the essay going and pulls it along; the cargo cars are the body (of whatever number needed to carry the information); and the caboose is the conclusion, signaling that the essay has come to an end. The couplings are the transitions (signal words) that both hold the ideas, words, sentences, and paragraphs together and show the relationships among those components. To see a sample of this train metaphor in slides, check the companion website for this book at http://teachingenglishlanguagearts.com.

WRITING AND EXPLORING VISUAL ARTS SUPPORT CONTENT LEARNING

Just as travelers often visit art museums to learn more about a community, town, or culture, you can invite your students to view and write about art as a way of learning and practicing exploratory writing. Ask students to choose a painting by one of the artists mentioned in a historical novel like *I, Juan de Pareja*, or one from the period or book you are teaching or they are studying in another course.

Selections may be chosen because they reflect artistic styles and cultures similar to those students already have seen or introduce something you plan to teach later. The goal is to offer a variety of paintings for students to view and make connections between experiences the students have had reading the literature or just living life. Begin with a common viewing experience, and then let students choose and write about their chosen piece of art or just their own way of writing about a common piece the class views together.

The following activities are based on notes from a workshop "Entering Art" led by Terry and Jenny Williams at the Detroit Institute of Art. Variations on these suggestions work to evoke inspiring student poetry as well as essays because art invites imaginative entry into its drama, mood, theme, locality, texture, and space. Both representational and abstract art can lure viewers into the artist's original act of creation. By all means, consult with the art teachers for suggestions appropriate for young students or are culturally accessible to students in your classes.

Entering Art and Writing about It

This imaginative entry evokes all five senses, memories, and dreams as students look and allow themselves to feel and imagine. Allow a full period for this assignment to give time for an experience that is personal and uniquely their own, and time to put experience into words that enrich both their own viewing and the work of art itself. And, so you can write along with your students, set the timer to ring five minutes before the end of the period to have time to debrief.

1. Have a large, sharp copy of the artwork projected when the students arrives in the classroom.
2. Play soft, lyric-free instrumental music as mood-creating background while students take their seats and you do beginning of the period record keeping.
3. Invite the students to join you in viewing the artwork silently for three minutes. Yes, three full minutes.
4. Then distribute the handout with the prompts you have chosen for the art you have.
5. Read each step aloud slowly and softly, pausing between prompts to allow time for students to look at the art and respond mentally.

Finally, invite the students to choose the kind of "entry" they would like to write about, and let them write for the next twenty minutes or so. Join in the experience and write along with your students. See textbox 5.1 for prompts adapted from my notes.

Invite your students to turn to a partner and read what they have written. It is revealing to have students who have viewed the same picture to read what they experienced.

You could extend this kind of exploring or writing and have your students use preselected website collections of art or photos like those on the Google Art Project or 24 Hours in Pictures. In the second instance, students could locate the photos taken on their own birth date. View all, choose one, and write about it.

This writing could be developed into a story, a poem, a dramatic scene, an explanation, a protest, a news article, a letter, or a speech. A copy of the art or photo on final draft could then be shared with class, posted on class website, and evaluated by teacher using customized Six Traits rubric created by student(s) doing the same genre to respond to the visual images. Their creating the rubric gives them ownership, but also reminds them of qualities expected in effective and interesting writing.

> **TEXTBOX 5.1**
> **ENTERING ART**
>
> 1. Step inside the artwork. Let its space become your space. What does it feel like as you journey into the painting? Where are you? What do you hear? Smell? What do you notice under your feet? Imagine you can touch something in the painting. What would that be? How would it feel?
> 2. Write about the artwork as if it were a dream. Bring the scene to life and leave us in that moment. Use "In a dream, I . . ." or "Last night I had the strangest dream . . ." or, simply, "I dreamed . . ."
> 3. Write about the scene as if it is happening now, using present tense and active verbs. Begin with "I am . . ." Move around inside the work and make things happen. Begin a line with "Suddenly . . ." in order to create surprise, moving into something unexpected.
> 4. Write about the work as if it is a memory. List short, separate memories or one long memory. Both invent and remember as you write.
> 5. Imagine the art as something you see outside a window. Begin with "From my window, I see . . ."

CONFERENCING TO CLARIFY STUDENT THINKING

> Art illuminates
> lessons we teach our students
> and they understand.
>
> —Anna J. Small Roseboro

No matter how well you have presented lessons or scheduled time for practice and review, sometimes only talking to individual students will ensure learning. One-on-one conferencing during the class time may be difficult to manage, but planning ahead can help you incorporate this valuable teaching strategy fairly early in the school year. Begin right away modeling ways to respond to writing. Then have students work for short periods of time in pairs, reading and responding to each other's drafts, and then as small groups in structured RAGs. Finally, perhaps by the second quarter, you can begin to integrate in-class conferencing with individual students.

When students experience the value of having your professional responses to their drafting, they may be patient enough to work independently, reading or writing, while you meet a few students each day in one-on-one conferences. The major reason for holding off scheduling in-class, one-on-one conferencing is not due to class management. It is to have time to build students' confidence in themselves and one another to become reliable readers and peer writing partners rather than relying solely on you. Knowing what can be expected also prepares them to come to conferences with good questions and open minds.

Until you can manage effective in-class conferencing, consider inviting students who wish to work in this way to meet with you before or after school or during their study periods. As the word gets around that getting one-on-one feedback from the teacher is helpful, students may be willing to cooperate in class, so they can also gain the benefits of this teaching/learning opportunity. In school settings with ready access to technology either at home or for all students to work on computers simultaneously in class, it is practical to teach students to do online peer responding as you work your way toward one-on-one conferencing. See the following chapters for optional ways to structure such an in-class activity.

Structure in-class time for one-to-one conferencing

It will take time to teach students how to use class time efficiently, so plan carefully and keep working toward this goal. Commend them when they do well with pairs and small group responding; continue to model and expect their cooperation. Often they respond just as they should.

Prepping for One-on-One Conferences

How do you prepare students for conferencing so that they will bring some insight into their own reading or writing process and remain open to taking something valuable from the conversation? One strategy is to have students come with specific written questions based on the assignment guideline. After they have done in-class prewriting to prime the pumps, written their first drafts to explore and organize their ideas, used the grading rubric to read and revise, participated in some form of peer feedback task like the one described in chapter 2, and written a second revision, it will be soon enough to schedule time for in-class conferencing.

If you get involved too soon, students may think all they have to do is follow your advice and earn an A. That erroneous idea seldom is the case when you use the general grading guidelines for which an A is awarded for the student's own creative touch. Most can accomplish a C; you can teach a B and only acknowledge the originality evident for the A. See the general grading guidelines diagram—figure 1.1—in chapter 1.

Gradually Add In-Class Conferencing

Your question may be about what the rest of the class should be doing while you conduct one-on-one conferences. Depending on the class makeup and what other assignments students have for the course, students could be doing independent reading, listening to audio books, and working on their handwritten or Word-processing drafts or revisions. Early on, it would not be unusual to be able to use only a portion of the period for conferences. Once the students become accustomed to them, you may be able to use the majority of the period because the students are coming prepared to work and wait. By then they are less uncomfortable with quiet on their side of the room and they are less distracted by the hushed conversation at the teacher's desk.

Consider returning final written drafts but withholding the grade until the students meet for the conference. Then they are more likely to pay attention to those time-consuming comments you have written as you read and decided the grade. In this case, students would come to the conference with one section of the paper revised and prepared to show how their revision improves their paper. You could begin the conference asking the student, "Based on the comments on the essay I returned to you, what grade do you think you earned?" Then have students show you the revised section, discuss the merits of that revision, and answer questions students may have.

To Grade or Not to Grade

The grade on the original essay should not be changed unless it is clear you made an error. Instead, encourage students to use what they learn in the conference when writing the next paper. Writing conferences themselves need not be graded, simply acknowledged with a check or plus in your grade book. These meetings serve as a formative assessment for you and your students to learn more about ways they view their own writing and ways they approach revisions.

You will find that keeping some notes about these conferences provides good information for parent conferences and questions from administrators, too. Having specific information about specific students demonstrates your attention to individuals that all three value: students, parents, and administrators. Time, patience, modeling, adapting, and adjusting by both the students and teacher ultimately lead to productive in-class conferencing.

TRAINING FOR SUCCESS

The first quarter at most schools is much like preseason training for sports teams. It is not that the athletes do not know the rules or no longer have the physical prowess to play the game; it is that they probably have not had to utilize that knowledge or those muscles during the off-season. It is much the same way with students and the reason teachers find themselves reviewing and reteaching what they know students have been taught before, not because the students do not know but because they have not been using what they had learned.

You know that for yourself. When you are preparing to teach a lesson, you are reviewing details about general topics you know you have known for years. What's that adage? If they don't use it, they'll lose it. Therefore, go ahead and reteach and then begin again to hold the students accountable for using what they are learning again.

CONCLUSION

It may take several weeks to cover the distance between reviewing informative writing to teaching persuasive writing. For some teachers, it takes the entire first three-quarters. Teaching and learning is a spiraling process. What they are trying themselves, students are likely to notice and point out during peer editing sessions. What they are discovering with your guidance is more lasting and useful than what they are simply shown or told.

As they explore with their peers, paying attention to features in the different texts, the emerging writers begin using this knowledge in their own reading and their own writing. By this time, your student traveling companions are prepared for the more sophisticated thinking required to write convincing arguments and persuasive essays and speeches as described in chapter 6, "Make the Case."

NOTES

1. "Blaise Pascal," Proverbia.net. 2009. http://en.proverbia.net/citastema.asp?tematica=888&page=2 (accessed July 6, 2012).
2. Jock Mackenzie, *Essay Writing: Teaching the Basics from the Ground Up* (Pembroke, NH: Pembroke Publishers, 2007).
3. English Language Arts Standards "Anchor Standards" *College and Career Readiness Anchor Standards for Writing.* 2012. http://www.corestandards.org/ELA-Literacy/CCRA/W/ (accessed June 23, 2018).

Chapter 6

Make the Case: Writing to Impact Thinking and Acting

> Reading maketh a full man, conference a ready man, and writing an exact man.
>
> —Sir Francis Bacon[1]

Looking back at what they have read is a good way to prepare students for what they are going to write. As Sir Francis Bacon's quotation suggests, when students have read, they are full and are ready to conference and talk with others about their thinking. They are eventually prepared to write with the kind of exact—precise and concise—language that leads to inviting reading by others. Oddly enough, this idea seems particularly true when teaching students how to write persuasive essays—ones that require writers to understand the audience they intend to influence about what they think and how they act.

Before readers are convinced to respond, they must be motivated. Taking time to look at motivation in the literature already studied this school year helps students understand what causes characters to change. Students then can use what they observe in their reading when they begin to write. Your younger students may not have the vocabulary yet, but probably mention during discussion that characters change when they believe refusing to do so will be dangerous, is illegal, is immoral, or will betray someone about whom they care deeply. If your students are ready, share the explanations that follow. If not, use general terms you know they will understand.

- *Beliefs*—what the character or audience accepts as fact—"The temperature is below freezing," "The Great Spirit created the universe."
- *Attitude*—what the character or audience believes about forces outside their control that makes the proposed change favorable/unfavorable or positive/

negative based on the character's beliefs—"My parents will never get me a . . .," "I'll be grounded if I go," "That group never liked me anyway."
- *Values*—the principles on which character or audience base their lives: moral codes, belief about what is right or wrong. In many cases, these relate to religion and politics—"It is dishonest to steal, even when you're hungry," "Never nark on a relative," "Our family always votes . . ."

Ask students to return to the text of readings you have studied together. Instruct your curious learners to seek out passages showing what the authors reveal about the beliefs, attitudes, and values of the characters. Then identify who or what in the story convinces the character that making a change in behavior would be a good or right thing to do. Remember, in many stories there are at least three attempts to solve the conflict in which the protagonist is embroiled, and usually the third, most difficult attempt involves a value's decision.

This same kind of looking at beliefs, attitudes, and values helps students read nonfiction, too. When they are asked to identify the tone of articles and essays, paying attention to words, phrases, and imagery the writers use to make their point, even the youngest middle school students discover what the writers seem to value. These close readings reveal the attitudes and behavior writers directly or indirectly invite or attempt to persuade the readers to adopt. As you select mentor texts for your writing assignments, consider those that your students can model as they write about topics that interest them.

What arguments tip the scales in favor of writer?

Make the Case

PRESENTING COMPELLING ARGUMENTS PRECEDES PERSUADING

A writer needs to know something about the readers to choose convincing facts and use compelling reasons that will be persuasive. Most students know this but may not realize they do. One effective way to illustrate this fact is to assign students to draft a letter persuading their parents or guardians to let them do something heretofore forbidden. This is an audience even immature middle school students know how to approach; they understand they must come up with both facts and reasons to get permission to do that forbidden thing and they must not finagle with the facts or use faulty reasoning.

Once students have giggled and guffawed about times they have gotten caught doing either of these things, go ahead and present a lesson on the ethics of argumentation. Keep it light, but keep it real. You may even share a story of your own.

Then, take them back a couple millennia and embellish your mini-lesson with the classical foundation of the art of rhetoric or honesty in arguing as attributed to Aristotle. You may find cartoons will keep it simple, while telling the story that, for eons, an essential part of a classical education has been learning to argue well. Your students readily accept as true that writers and speakers who can convince the audience to change are the ones who rise to become leaders in the school, community, nation, and even the world. Invite them to name such leaders they know about from history, movies, and current events.

The effective writer/speaker is one who knows the audience well, appeals to their feelings, and explains with reasons that benefit the individuals in that audience. Such knowledgeable writers consistently convince their listeners to change their ways. However, those more respected writers and orators are those who can be trusted to act with integrity. They are those men and women who resist the temptation to twist evidence and use sloppy reasoning. That is the kind of honesty you strive to instill in your students.

UNVEILING ARISTOTLE'S ART OF RHETORIC

Go ahead and use the Greek words "ethos," "pathos," and "logos." These are premium root words for students to know because they make up many words in the academic vocabulary middle school students encounter now or will in the future. In addition, the students will feel so sophisticated using them when they brag to their family and friends what they learned from you.

No need to belabor the points or require students to memorize the definitions of each Greek term. The purpose is to show that what they are studying now has been a part of education curricula since the time of _____ !

(use whatever hyperbolic term for a long, long, long time ago, which will impress your students): the gladiators; time of Christ; ancient Chinese dynasties, or when Abraham, Mohammed, or the Buddha lived.

VIEWING ENHANCES UNDERSTANDING

Just a couple more steps before sending the students off to write effective persuasive essays on their own. Bring in print, media, and digital advertisements to show students ways that they—yes, even your most astute ones—are persuaded to buy clothes, food, games, and sugary drinks. As students view commercials that manipulate prospective customers, the students develop an understanding about ethos, pathos, and logos more quickly than simply hearing the terms defined.

If time permits, you could present a lesson about fallacies that include bandwagoning, hasty generalization, snob appeal, slippery slope, and appeal to authority. Even young teens will be able to recognize these in advertisements they see online, on television, and in magazines. They just may not know the names. Teaching them arms students to become not only more critical consumers of media but also more conscientious constructing it.

SPARRING TO LISTEN FOR SOUND ARGUMENTS

Practicing aloud arguments and attempts to persuade is an effective way to prepare students for writing strong, convincing essays. Consider conducting SPARs (spontaneous arguments) in class, which are based on everyday topics, such as which is better, more nutritious, more popular, more useful, more economical, and more fun than something else. What should be required or banned?

Two pairs of students debate one another for about ten minutes per topic. They must include facts and not just opinions to be convincing. This is an exciting way to teach presenting, listening, and responding to opposing views on topics appropriate for middle school and culturally diverse discussions. See lessons on the companion website for this book at www.teachingenglishlanguagearts.com.

- Team A: Speaker 1 draws a topic from a hat or a bowl, announces it to the class, and then has just a couple minutes to prepare and then present a case for making a change.
- Team B: Speaker 1, the opposing team, must address each argument presented by the first speaker and then within the two or three minutes counter each argument with his or her own.

- Team A: Speaker 2 then offers a rebuttal, or response, to those challenges.
- Team B: Speaker 2 sums up the arguments for that side and calls for action.

The audience decides who presents the more convincing case by voting anonymously on a prepared ballot. Then a second set of students comes to the front, draws, and presents arguments for their topic. Usually three rounds at a time suffice to demonstrate the value of listening and responding with logical reasons. A structure that may help the SPARers stay on task says as follows:

- *Name* it: what's the problem or issue?
- *Explain* it: show why this is a problem or issue of concern for the audience.
- *Prove* it: use factual evidence, not just the opinion of speaker.
- *Conclude* it: ("Therefore . . .") state a good reason to consider the alternative view or to make a change.

Students are likely to notice how similar this is to the PIE structure where writers state their POSITION, offer ILLUSTRATIONS that show and exemplify the position, and then EXPLAIN link(s) between the two. Still, it should not be surprising that it takes several attempts at SPARring for students to learn the structure and stay on task without erupting into side arguments. This is hard work that requires attentive listening and disciplined thinking.

The value of SPARring is that students hear how important it is to counter opposing views without insulting the intelligence of the reader/audience. If the writer/speaker does not appear to respect the fact that the other side has valid reasons for holding to those beliefs or behaviors, the reader/audience is likely to close down and stop reading or listening. Be prepared. You may have to admonish your students that volume does not convince; practical solutions do.

WRITING ABOUT ISSUES THAT MATTER

If you would persuade, you must appeal to interest rather than intellect.

—Benjamin Franklin[2]

Students are more enticed to learn when they see an immediate purpose for doing so. It, therefore, makes sense to assign the persuasive essays in conjunction with current events that take place on your school site, in the community, in the state, or in the world. A worthwhile reason for students to use their newly crafted skills is to write letters to persuade someone to change a policy or a law. Students can use the same strategies for writing these letters or articles as they did to write letters to their parents or guardians.

You get more buy-in from the students when you resist the temptation to force the whole class to write about the same topic or on one that is important only to you. If they have no passion for the topic, students are likely to resist giving it their all as they plan and are less likely to write credible essays that answer these kinds of questions:

- What is the problem?
- What does the audience believe or feel about the problem? How do you know?
- What has the audience said or done to show that is what they believe or feel?
- What should be done to solve the problem? How do you know?
- Which arguments will appeal to the head (facts), the heart (emotions), and the pocket (financial cost)?
- Why will a change in belief or action benefit the audience?
- How will life be better once the change is in place?

Now that they have a better understanding of knowing their audience, marshaling their facts, articulating reasons for change, and practicing countering arguments, students are ready to write more nuanced essays zoning in on the

Students read and insert comments online

specific purpose that will compel their readers to take notice and maybe even take action and become part of the solution.

CAREFUL STEPS TO EFFECTIVE WRITING

> Don't get it right.
> Get it written,
> Then get it right.
>
> —George Moberg[3]

Students sometimes wonder how they can make a well-written early draft even better. If you teach them specific steps they can take to improve their writing, you will have taught something they can use for life. Consider using alliteration to help them recall the tasks that can be done in any order. During revision, encourage students to do the following:

- *Expand:* develop what is written to make ideas clearer and more interesting without being repetitive. Add more information to show rather than tell. Use carefully chosen examples from literature (any reading and viewing), life (personal experiences and observations) and lessons learned in other content area courses.
- *Explain:* clarify what is written by using various reasons based on experiences, observations, and lessons learned in other courses.
- *Exchange and rearrange:* ask what words can be substituted to make the writing clearer, more interesting, and more precise. Substitute abstract nouns with more concrete nouns, more words that have the positive or negative connotations to create the desired mood in your reader. Think about ways words, sentences, and paragraphs can be rearranged to make the ideas unfold more smoothly, making the writer's thoughts clearer, more interesting, and inviting to consider.
- *Expunge:* get rid of distracting or weak words, phrases, and sentences that cloud writing and prevent ideas from shining through, glowing with authority as they inform, convince, persuade, and even entertain.
- *Enliven:* consider using more active verbs instead of passive ones in forms of the verb "to be."

EVALUATING AND WRITING ABOUT PUBLISHED WRITING

Adolescent readers sometimes wonder why teachers get so excited about books, plays, poems, essays, and films that do not seem all that appealing to young people. They may not understand until you point out that each reader has his or her own standards to measure what is interesting or worth reading.

SHARE CRITERIA FOR MEASURING RESPONSE TO READING

You can demonstrate this fact by sharing a set of criteria for evaluating literature and establish a valuable prelude to students writing thoughtful evaluations of literature and film. The results will provide evidence your students are reaching the standards measuring that they know how to write their own thoughtful considerations of different aspects of print, digital, and film media. Working as a class, ask your students to score their response to a piece of literature they already have studied together. Try to mask your own opinions as they add their comments talking about the following:

1. *Clarity*: how easy or difficult the text or film was to understand when they read or viewed.
2. *Escape*: how much they found themselves drawn away from their everyday life as they read the text or viewed.
3. *Reflection of real life*: how much the people and places seemed familiar or at least some reflection of life as the student knows it.
4. *Artistry in Details*: did they find that, though difficult at times, the writing or filming seemed to be artistic and interesting enough to reread/review just to bask in the beauty of the setting or to relive the terror created by the author's skillful use of sparkling vocabulary, fresh images, realistic dialogue, interesting words in a fresh and engaging way? The same may be considered about the director's use of camera angles and shots, lighting, and music.
5. *Internal Consistency*: if the text and film flows well and all parts seem to fit into a meaningful way, some readers will give the work high marks. On the other hand, if either seems disjointed or has scenes that could be deleted without being missed, these evaluators will give the piece low marks.
6. *Tone*: sometimes readers respond positively or negatively to something read or viewed because they appreciate how well an author's tone, personal style, or attitude comes through the writing. That may be one of the reasons adolescents enjoy a book and its film series so much.
7. *Emotion*: they know what to expect and look forward to experiencing the work of one who clearly reveals one's feelings about a topic. Some readers rate high the literature or film that creates a strong emotional response whether it is a positive or negative one. The moods created may be lasting and universal.

8. *Personal Beliefs*: in another vein, the writing may be appealing to certain readers simply because it confirms their personal beliefs. Even if they cannot put it into words, novice as well as veteran readers are influenced by their own ideas relating to religion, politics, social issues—attitudes about what is moral or immoral, right or wrong.
9. *Significant Insight*: perhaps the quality of literature and film that is more difficult to articulate relates to its ability to provide a window and mirror to life, offering new insight into other individuals, groups, places, and situations. The writing or film may compel those who experience it to consider their own behaviors and thoughts about life and death, good and evil.

Works that unveil what is true and beautiful and prick our conscience to become better people are those texts and films that are widely read and viewed for years and years. It is this significant insight derived from published works that spurs educators to teach the classics even though students seldom appreciate their value until years later.[4]

CHART OF RESPONSES PROVIDES DATA FOR WRITING

You and your students may come up with more sophisticated terminology for evaluating literature and film, but you can get your student evaluators started just using the phrases that follow. They can use these nine lenses to organize their thoughts on the value of what they read and view. Ask them to rate each criterion on a scale of 1–5 (low to high). (See figure 6.1)

1. Easy to understand (clarity)
2. Takes me away from now (escape)
3. Seems like real people and places (reflection)
4. Creative writing/filming worth revisiting (artistry)
5. Parts fit together well (internal consistency)
6. Author's/director's opinions seem obvious (tone)
7. Creates strong feelings (emotional)
8. Morals match mine (personal)
9. Challenges me to think about others with compassion (significance)

As students record their responses, remind them to include in their notes specific references to the text or film. They will need those examples to flesh out their evaluative review in discussion and/or writing. During the whole class mini-lesson about the common text, invite students to quote a short phrase or sentence; suggest key words as examples; and identify page numbers, paragraph numbers, or reference to specific scenes.

Nine YARDSTICKS of Value

Yardstick	1	2	3	4	5
Clarity					
Escape					
Reflection					
Artistry					
Internal Consistency					
Tone					
Emotional					
Personal					
Significance					

Figure 6.1. "Nine Yardsticks" helps students evaluate text
Source: Blair and Gerber (1959)

ORGANIZE NOTES FOR REVEALING CRITIQUES

Once they have their prewriting notes, your critics are ready to think about how to pull them all together into a well-structured piece of argumentative writing that explains why they evaluated the experience the way they have. Questions to consider are the following:

- What is your *general response* to this piece of literature or film? Strong, moderate, or weak?
- Why have you *ranked* the work as you have?
- What specific references from the literary work or film can you *cite to explain and support* your opinion? Which quotations will best show what you want to say?

Next, your students get to decide the best way to organize their thoughts. They could write about the following:

- strong qualities to weak—those that rate highest to those that rate lowest;
- more personal qualities to less personal ones;
- vice versa; or
- some other way.

The class may need to be reminded to include in the opening paragraph the title and author of the work as well as their general response to the literature. This will be an opinion word, an adjective or adverb that will guide their writing and alert their reader about what will follow. The evaluation may begin with a carefully selected quotation that reflects the strong point the student writer will explore and expand in the remainder of the critique.

Together, once you introduce this way of looking at text and film, look at reviews of literature found on the back of paperback books, on library leaflets, and on websites that sell books or video. These models may be a good start for your students. They soon see that many of the published reviewers and film critics include references directly or indirectly to each of the criteria just as you are asking your students to consider.

After creating a chart of their responses and looking at sample critiques, your students should be ready to write their own. These can provide written evidence of their ability to develop a fully developed essay that persuasively shows their deep reading and careful consideration of many aspects of a published work they have read or film they have viewed.

This evaluative writing may be adapted to writing in science and social studies. Students could be asked to reflect on application of science or technology, historical documents, or descriptions of incidents in history. You know your students, what you are teaching, and what learning you need to measure. Adapt as needed to achieve your goals.

WRITING FOR A SPECIFIC AUDIENCE

Invite students to choose a topic on something that interests them or that they are studying in another class. This will reinforce or expand their thinking about this other topic and earn them credit for completing an assignment in your class. For some students, it can be an efficient way to spend the next couple of weeks.

This is an opportune time to remind your students about audience and the kind of language they can use to best get their ideas across. For example, if they choose to argue about reducing injuries in a particular sport and are speaking to sports fans, the writer is right to use sports-specific jargon and slang. To demonstrate this fact, ask your students what this sentence means: "The difficulty of your set could be increased if you do a jam followed by a peach." Class members familiar with gymnastics will understand the speaker is describing the point value of a gymnastics routine. The sentence means that the point values you can earn on your gymnastics routine can be bigger if you include, in sequence, two particular skills on the uneven parallel bars: the "jam," which leaves the gymnast sitting on the high bar; and the "peach," where the gymnast moves from the high bar to the low bar.

If, on the other hand, the essay is being written to be delivered at a school board meeting comprised of neighbors from many walks of life, the writer would choose the more general language likely to be understood by audience less familiar with the lingo of the sport and include explanations when that lingo is spoken. The same care in choosing language would be true if the student is writing about dance, music, or art or to an audience familiar with a specific culture or event. In each case, the prior knowledge of the audience with the topic should determine the language the writer chooses to use in the final text version of the essay, article, or letter. See chapter 10 for ways these strategies work in speeches.

WRITING FROM RESEARCH: A SUMMATIVE ASSESSMENT

Want to introduce students to different kinds of basic reference resources? During the second quarter of the school year, design a series of mini-lessons that point out a range of reference materials that published writers use. Consider how often one sees definitions, quotations, anecdotes, personal experience, and references to current events in editorials and speeches. Middle school students are familiar with dictionaries and newspapers and magazines but may not know about collections of quotations and anecdotes. Young writers know they are supposed to acknowledge when they borrow information from others but may not have had many assignments that ask them to show that they know how to do this.

Consider a short writing assignment that requires that they do just that. They could write an editorial on an abstract term and then present those ideas in an informal speech and show how well they are progressing on meeting standards in reading, writing, speaking, and listening. Of particular focus is the writing standard that requires students to "gather relevant information from multiple print and digital sources, assess the credibility and accuracy of each source, and integrate the information while avoiding plagiarism."[5]

WRITING ABOUT AN ABSTRACT TERM

In this writing-speaking assignment, students can draw from a hat an abstract term like those in the chart in figure 6.2. Then from the specified resources, gather information to write an editorial that can be converted into a short persuasive speech designed to raise the awareness of their readers and listeners about their chosen term. The editorial and speech should give significant reasons to strive to achieve or to avoid an experience with the abstract idea like those in the list.

Make the Case 83

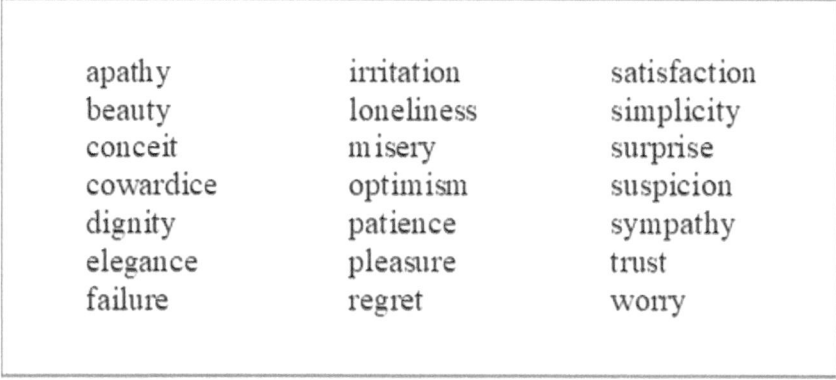

Figure 6.2. Research and write about abstract terms

Adjust the list to meet the language skills of your students. It is fine for more than one student to have the same term and makes for interesting reading to see how different students handle the same word. Have students work in pairs, and add a visual component where students include a collage or a set of five to six slides to supplement their oral presentation. The primary goals are to learn about and use a variety of resources in a persuasive writing. The final presentation should include five of the following six kinds of support:

1. Definition of chosen term
2. Quotation using the term
3. Anecdote—could be an example from texts read together in class
4. Some sort of statistic or number relating to their term
5. Personal experience or observation of the term in action
6. Contemporary issue or situation illustrating the term

Of course, students will be expected to cite their sources, so this assignment can be a fine summative assessment of a variety of skills you are required to teach. It will be helpful to know which citation style is used in your district high school—Chicago, MLA, APA, or another. Students with knowledge of citations will be better prepared for the academic challenges in whatever writing they do in the future.

REVIEWING AND INTRODUCING REFERENCE RESOURCE MATERIALS

To assure that students are prepared for this complex assignment, consider a series of mini-lessons reviewing ways to use each of the resources. Your students may have had experience with some of the reference materials and simply forgotten a few finer points. For example, they know a dictionary is a collection of words with entries containing definitions but may not recall what all the symbols and abbreviations mean.

For the print dictionary, direct student attention to the guide words at the top of the pages that help them determine whether the word they are searching will appear on that page. It is particularly helpful to English language learners to know that some online dictionaries include pronunciation guides with familiar words to help decide how to say the vowels and diphthongs, as well as hyperlinks to hear the word pronounced so viewers can hear and practice saying it.

Both print and digital dictionaries include many common features. Most will have phonetic spellings in parentheses; a letter to indicate the part of speech; and what the word means when used as a noun, a verb, an adjective, or an adverb. Many dictionaries include a phrase or sentence showing how the word is used. More extensive entries also include the etymology of the words. (Good time to mention value of knowing root words.)

You should be able to locate several websites with lessons to help you plan one just right for your students. Some of the sites even have quizzes to test student understanding before you move on to next reference resource.

Compelling Arguments

Appeal to head...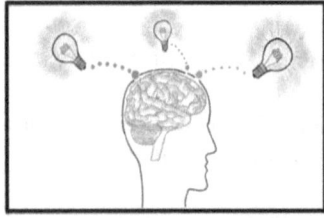

...heart...

...and pocket.

If your students do not have consistent access to online resources, borrow print dictionaries and books with collected quotations from the school and community libraries and from your colleagues. From the collection of quotations, students should find one that includes their abstract term. A well-chosen quotation can illustrate or drive home the point the students want to make about their specific term.

USE STORIES AND STATISTICS
TO APPEAL TO THE HEART AND HEAD

After explaining to your students that anecdotes are usually short narrations of an interesting, amusing, or biographical incident, share a couple of your favorites. They should be brief enough to be told in thirty to forty-five seconds and can be chosen to appeal to the heart and therefore be convincing. Show your eager listeners how these little stories can further explain or demonstrate a point a writer or speaker is trying to make. Encourage them to listen for such stories in other settings—other classes, political events, worship settings.

If your students are recent English language learners, you may find it useful to find a translation or "anecdote" in their native language or culture. Many students will recognize this strategy for clarifying and driving home a point. A lesson on anecdotes is a culturally responsive way to invite students to share teaching stories their families tell.

Statistics may be a challenge for students to find. But because many readers and listeners are more impressed by numbers, using statistics ethically can be a powerful persuasive strategy that appeals to the head and the heart. Students are familiar with statistics in sports, movies, and music and on commercials that relate percentages about the number of people who use or are impacted by certain products.

Young teens often are enticed to do or buy something if it will put them in the group of the popular majority. Advertisers often use bandwagoning—the suggestion that everyone is doing it. It can be a persuasive appeal that uses specific numbers. From their studies in science and social studies, students already may be familiar with the use of numbers to make a point in terms of ecology and demographics. Invite your budding researchers to use numbers from one of those commercials or classes if they will work in their article and speech.

CONNECT TO CURRENT EVENTS

Requiring that their writing and speech include evidence based on a contemporary issue or situation is a good reason to teach students how to read and extrapolate information from print or digital news articles. In any case, students should pay attention to current events and chose one that illustrates a reason to strive for or to avoid an experience with their abstract term. Remind them to record when and where they get their facts.

No matter how limited the electronic resources available to your students, it is important to teach them the basics of citing resources as a matter of academic honesty. Whatever they borrow should be acknowledged. For young, inexperienced students, you may simplify the task by requiring only a list of resources consulted—a list of the websites, books, articles from which students borrow information for use in their writing or speaking. The minimum list should be a dictionary, a source for quotation, anecdote, statistic, and current event. You can ask the students to alphabetize the list by author or title.

For older, more experienced students, teach them how to write endnotes, where they include in the text of their writing a number that links what has been borrowed to a specific article or book with the same number in addition to a bibliography or list of sources consulted. Include on your websites links to sites with samples and tutorials for creating citations. This is valuable for three reasons: students have access when they need it; they will not have to keep asking you, using valuable class time; and it will reduce grading time because more assignments will be written and cited correctly because students will have checked citations during peer editing steps.

ORGANIZING THE RESEARCHED INFORMATION

Once you have introduced and reviewed these resources and given students time to practice using them, give the abstract term assignment. Here are some guidelines to help them organize their writing.

Introduction

- Dramatic opening that links to the idea of the article/speech—could begin with anecdote, quotation, or startling statistic
- Transition to signpost—two or three sentences that link opening ideas to their purpose/thesis/signpost statement
- Purpose/thesis/signpost statement—shows writer/speaker will follow a specific organizational pattern in the body of article/speech, such as:
  - *chronological*: in order of time
  - *cause and effect*: tell about a problem and the effect of it
  - *order of importance*: most important idea to least, or visa versa
  - *problem and solution*: describe a problem and offer solution

Body

- Incorporate five of the six kinds of evidence listed earlier
- Appropriate transitions (refer to list of transitions/signal words)
- Anything else the writer/speaker thinks will make article/speech more interesting to read or hear

Conclusion

- Memorable closing: could save quotation for closing
- Summary of key ideas
- Challenge to attain or avoid experience with the idea of the abstract term
- Call for change: urging reader/listener to strive to attain or avoid experience with the term

Students should be encouraged to draft their article/speech using these guidelines but be free to adjust during the revision stages.

PLAN TIME FOR GIVING AND PROCESSING PEER FEEDBACK

Another version for designing lessons for students to read and comment on the writing of their peers follows here. In this case, students may comment in class or for homework. You could have five color-coded groups, and students can choose to respond to any three members in their assigned group: red to blue, blue to green, green to orange, orange to purple, purple to yellow, and yellow to red.

In class, based on the length and skill of your readers, set the timer for eight to ten minutes to read each paper. Review the rubric first; then let them begin reading.

- Classmate A: *content* sufficient to meet requirements of assignment
- Classmate B: *structure* of essay, of paragraphs, of sentences
- Classmate C: *language, quality of resources* or *evidence, mugs* (mechanics, usage, grammar, spelling), and so on.

You may decide to use a version of the basic or customized Six Traits Writing Rubric and organize responses based on those. This time students respond to as follows:

- Classmate A: traits 1 and 4
- Classmate B: traits 2 and 5
- Classmate C: traits 3 and 6

After the third buzzer, have students open and read comments on their own papers, write a three-step plan for revision, "I will improve content, organization, language, etc., by _____ ," and send it to you by e-mail, if students are working online, or show it to you before the period ends, if handwritten.

In both peer feedback versions, students read three different drafts and receive feedback from three different readers. After you have modeled highlighting and inserting comments, students usually can handle this task with ease. They see what works and what does not and maybe even notice ways to improve their own work as they use the same rubric or grading guidelines as you will use to evaluate their writing. Practice these strategies for giving and receiving feedback in class two or three before assigning for homework. Once you are certain students know how to navigate the programs, you can be confident their work will go smoothly outside of class.

Many students look forward to the opportunity to give and receive feedback before they revise again. You can view their comments, give them credit for participating in this writing process step, and see what issues need to be addressed in next class meeting. Allotting time for in-class peer feedback and revision is worth class time. Better writing accrues, and you can spend less time grading.

CONCLUSION

It may take several weeks to make the trip from reviewing informative writing to teaching persuasive writing. For some teachers it takes the entire school year. However, for you who knows where you are heading, the expedition does not seem interminable as long as you are confident that you have not gotten lost.

Stop occasionally to rest and enjoy the side trips that confirm the value of teaching different modes of writing. Look at ways published writers and speakers use the skills you are teaching. Invite students to bring in examples they see in other classes, in their own independent reading, or even to point them out in the fiction and nonfiction you study together in class. Craft lessons for students to model what they read and view.

By the final quarter of the school year, on the last few miles of the journey, the students will be more confident and competent persuasive communicators because they understand the purpose of different kinds of writing, and they appreciate ethics of argumentation, the value of organization, and the importance of respecting their reader/audience. Equally important, your maturing students will have become more critical readers and listeners, more alert to ways others may use these skills to convince readers/listeners/viewers to change their beliefs and behavior. The lessons in chapter 10 demonstrate ways to adapt these lessons to writing to speak. For, now, read on to explore ways to verse life writing poetry and drama.

NOTES

1. Francis Bacon, "Essays of Francis Bacon—Of Studies." Authorama Public Domain Books. http://en.proverbia.net/citastema.asp?tematica=888&page=2 (accessed January 1, 2018).
2. "Benjamin Franklin, Mind Quotes," *Finest Quotes*. http://izquotes.com/quote/283028 (accessed January 1, 2018).
3. Goran "George" Moberg, *Writing in Groups: New Techniques for Good Writing without Drills*, 3rd ed. (New York: The Writing Consultant, 1984).
4. Adapted from the writing of Walter Blair and John Gerber in their 1959 textbook *Literature*, published by Scott Foresman.
5. Common Core Anchor Standards. http://www.corestandards.org/ELA-Literacy/CCRA/W/8/ (accessed July 3, 2018).

Chapter 7

Verse Life Together: Reading and Writing Poetry

> Robert, Bobby, Bob
> Fast, fleet, flown
> Baby, boy, grown
>
> —Anna J. Small Roseboro, "Our Son"

Even if your students are on board and initially excited about reading and talking about poetry and plays, you may soon face a roadblock when you ask them to write it. Why? Perhaps because reading poetry can be such a challenging experience. Students may not think that they are "deep" enough to write poetry. True, some students are naturally talented poets, but others learn by seeing how others write, being inspired or patterning the work of others. This probably is the best reason to read and study a variety of samples before assigning all your students to write poetry to be graded as a genre. Once they understand the unique characteristics of these genres and experience the joy of word play by others, they more eagerly accept the challenge to try versing, writing poems and short plays of their own.

Like many teachers, you probably have been reading poems and having students write poetry as part of other lessons already. You may have had students write verse in response to literature or historical events because you understand what a fine vehicle poetry is for showcasing young writers' understanding of their reading and its connection to their lives.

Now, in this chapter, notice that the purpose of writing poetry is different. It is for your students to experiment and conscientiously apply some of the literary devices to recreate experiences of their own, while meeting the curriculum and English language arts standards that ask students to demonstrate anchor tasks like:

- producing clear and coherent writing in which the development, organization, and style are appropriate to task, purpose, and audience;
- developing and strengthening writing as needed by planning, revising, editing, rewriting, or trying a new approach; and
- using technology, including the Internet, to produce and publish writing, and to interact and collaborate with others.[1]

This chapter takes you and your students traveling into interesting side paths and offers suggestions for trying out different approaches to poetry writing and performing. Therefore, feel free to let the students get off the school bus for a while and play with the language. Invite them to splash around in freshwater streams; to wallow around in the mud a bit, manipulating words, forms, and imagery; to wander through the open markets checking out the collections you gathered to show how published writers craft their poems, sampling the goods, and trying on styles; and to experiment a bit, tasting different cuisines—all before you begin evaluating the quality of your students' writing.

Choose from the following activities and adapt them with those you know. Design lessons to help students compose a variety of poems that reflect

Teaching poetry can be challenging

their own personal experiences and observations, and encourage them to dig deeper into quality published literature.

PATTERNING AND EMULATING POEMS

Want a compelling way for your reluctant writers to jump into poetry writing? Imitation: modeling what others write. This is nothing new. Patterning and copying the work of others are traditional ways to learn difficult skills. Consider the painter and musician, the dancer and athlete. In each case, novices try to duplicate the strokes and colors, the sound and technique, the form and movement of the masters. You can give your students similar opportunities during this poetry unit.

Lead the way and model for them. First, choose a poem that you love and, with your curious students watching, show how you work through the process of figuring out the pattern and then of imitating that pattern. Ask them to look for rhyme and rhythm; draw their attention to the layout of lines and sentence structure; entice them to imitate the kinds of imagery; or challenge them to recreate the emotional impact using words chosen for sounds and connotation.

Perhaps you already are familiar with the poem, "Where I'm From" by George Ella Lyon or "The Delight Song of Tsoai-Talee" by Scott Momaday. Use poems like these to begin, and let the students pick one or two of their favorite poems from the books on hand or online. Then have them write a poem that emulates the structure, style, techniques, and rhythm of their chosen poet. For specific assignment handouts, see the companion website for this book at www.teachingenglishlanguagearts.com.

Structured poems may be your choice to introduce this kind of poetry writing. The limerick, the haiku, and the sonnet are traditional patterns of poetry, each with a specific rhyme or rhythm pattern. Many of your students already are familiar with these patterns from elementary school. Following, are a couple traditional patterns to trigger their memory.

Limerick

A limerick is a five-line poem, usually funny, that follows an AABBA rhyme pattern;

> There was an Old Man in a tree,
> Who was horribly bored by a Bee;
> When they said, "Does it buzz?"
> He replied, "Yes, it does!"
> "It's a regular brute of a Bee!"
>
> —Edward Lear[2]

How about having your music lovers pattern song lyrics? You may find useful ideas from MUSIC (Musicians United for Songs in the Classroom), Inc., *Learning from Lyrics* website.

While you definitely want to spend some time modeling the different poems with or for your students, save plenty of time for them to experiment independently. Remember, your goal is to provide structure and cultivate a safe and relaxed setting to experiment. Slowly but steadily release some of that control to the students.

The way you spend time shows what is important. During this portion of the unit, play and practice are important. Soon you can persuade them to perform their self-selected or original poems for their peers. And just as athletes and dancers who practice a lot feel more confident performing, your maturing writers feel more assured when they have practiced.

Pantoums—Repeating Lines Make the Poem

One pattern that yields successful poems is the less-familiar pantoum, a poem consisting of eight non-rhyming lines; each is used twice. Less intimidating for reluctant poets, the pantoum is based more on repetition that on rhyme or rhythm patterns. It can be used as an alternative book report to capture key events—a memorable scene, a favorite character from a literary work, or a life experience—or lessons learned in another class. Anne Brown's seventh-grade class finished reading an autobiographical book written primarily in free verse, "*Brown Girl Dreaming*," by Jacqueline Woodson, and drafted this pantoum as a class activity. Note the simple instructions in italics:

Begin by writing four original lines:

(1) A girl named Jackie
(2) In a country divided by race
(3) Moved from North to South
(4) Living with the blanket of her grandparents love

Repeat lines two and four, and add lines five and six to expand ideas introduced in lines two and four, like this:

(2) In a country divided by race
(5) Two siblings and one parent in a long ride "home"
(4) Living with the blanket of her grandparents love
(6) Buried five days a week giving witness to Jehovah

Repeat lines five and six, and add lines seven and eight to expand ideas mentioned in lines five and six, like this:

(5) Two siblings and a parent in a long ride "home"
(7) Anchored in childhood by candy on Friday and ribbons on Sunday
(6) Buried five days a week giving witness to Jehovah
(8) Moving again, New York City, new sibling, new life

Finally, repeat lines one, three, seven, and eight in this order:

(7) Anchored in childhood by candy on Friday and ribbons on Sunday
(3) Moved from North to South
(8) Moving again, New York City, new sibling, new life
(1) A girl named Jackie

The result is a lovely poem that captures the essence of the story. As you read and then write your own sample of this pattern poem, you can see how much grammar, usage, and punctuation students must employ to make sure pronouns are the right number and gender and that the verbs are the right tense to make sense as they add more lines! You can bet Ms. Brown had her

Poetry captures personal experiences and observations

students do just that when they looked back and saw some of the issues they missed when they were drafting.

Consider having students write pantoums about a series of math concepts, science discoveries, or historical personages or incidents—a great way to review and summarize before a summative assessment.

Lazy Sonnets: Just Fourteen Words

Here is a streamlined structured format that works well with ninth-grade students and gutsy younger ones. You may assign these "lazy sonnets" after a formal study of poetry that includes lessons on the traditional fourteen-line sonnets, after teaching Shakespeare's *Romeo and Juliet* or another play that includes sonnets. The only rules are to use fourteen words and to follow, in the closing verse, the rhyme pattern of an Elizabethan (Shakespearean) or Italian (Petrarchan) sonnet.

As a culminating activity following a study of a text, invite the students simply to encapsulate a key idea and show the characters, conflicts, or a theme of the fiction or nonfiction piece. You could divide the class into five groups, one per act, or a number that fits the play you are studying and then have students in each group write about their assigned act or section of text. See table 7.1 for a lazy sonnet on the left by Kaveh based on Act V of *Romeo and Juliet* by William Shakespeare. On the right is a lazy sonnet written in Nancy Himel's class when studying, the lyrical ballad, "The Rime of the Ancient Mariner," by Samuel Taylor Coleridge.

Table 7.1. Lazy Sonnets as Summaries

Romeo and Juliet, Act V	"The Rime of the Ancient Mariner"
Paris slain by Romeo.	Mariner shoots. Albatross dies.
Romeo then slew himself.	Storms blow. Crew dies.
Later Juliet slew herself.	Mariner prays. Penance granted:
Madness Sadness	Hoary story.

What is particularly fun about writing these lazy sonnets is that they are manageable for a range of students. Your creative students may write quickly enough to enter their sonnets on the computer and print out these unrevised sonnets by the end of the period. Quick. Fun. Enlightening for students. Revealing to you.

CAPTURING PERSONAL EXPERIENCES IN POETRY ADDS AUTHENTICITY

Much writing is autobiographical, portraying personal experiences. But it can be more. Joseph Epstein writes, "The personal essay is, in my experience, a form of discovery. What one discovers in writing such essays is where one stands on complex issues, problems, questions, and subjects. In writing the essay, one tests one's feelings, instincts, and thoughts in the crucible of composition."[3] This self-discovery is also true when versing life in poetry.

For their poetry assignments, encourage but do not require students to use their personal experiences and observations as they imitate the structure and pattern of published poetry they enjoy. In keeping with the philosophy of the National Writing Project, write along with your students. This keeps you attuned to what it feels like to write "on demand" and gives you an opportunity to reveal to your students a little of who you are when you are not teaching.

You probably recall from attending poetry readings yourself that poets often explain the incident that gave rise to their poem. I did that for my poem inspired by Robert Frost's "I Have Been One Acquainted with the Night." Here is what I gave as background for the poem.

A PERSONAL STORY

In 1996, I was a part of a team of teachers who, sponsored by Rotary International, served as ambassadors of education to Kenya, Uganda, and the French island of Mauritius. I had never been to Africa and was thrilled about the opportunity and also a little apprehensive.

Families in Africa who were curious about us and about our country hosted us in their homes. On our last evening in Mombasa, Kenya, our hosts threw a large lawn party. After dinner, they asked our team to speak about our time in Mombasa. When I arose to speak, trying to compose myself and gather my thoughts, I looked up. Seeing the brilliant night sky, it suddenly struck me that I could be standing on the soil of my ancestors; they could have stood in this same place and witnessed such a sparkly navy blanket of a sky.

As a fifth-generation descendent of African slaves, I have no idea where my family originated. Nevertheless, standing under the Kenyan night, tears leaked from my eyes; primordial memories arose and clogged my throat; I couldn't see; I couldn't speak, but somehow I began to sing the old Negro Spiritual, "Sometimes I Feel

Like a Motherless Child." To this day, I have no idea why that particular song came to me. Nor did I realize how deeply lodged in my memory that experience had become—until I began patterning Robert Frost's poem "I Have Been One Acquainted with the Night." It was then that I understood Epstein's point that writing is a form of discovery.

Describing my African experience did help my students understand that we humans often do not know what we think or feel until we read what we write. I encourage you to write with your students, too. You, too, may unlock something memorable about an experience you have had and may write a poem you are willing to share with your students. Here is mine.

> I have been one acquainted with that song.
> I've sung the song in tune—and out of tune
> I have held that high note oh so long.
>
> I have sung the song—clear like a loon.
> I have kept within the music's beat
> And swooped down low, yet staying right in tune.
>
> I've sung that song and let my voice just soar
> While deep within my soul the words brought tears
> That slipped right down my cheeks; my heart just tore.
>
> That song, reminding me of trials sore
> Experienced by people who did so long
> For freedom, justice, rights, and so much more.
> Freedoms they'd awaited far too long.
> I have been one acquainted with that song.
>
> —Anna J. Small Roseboro, "Acquainted with That Song," patterned after "Acquainted with the Night," by Robert Frost.

Initially, you may be uncomfortable writing about your personal experiences in front of or along with your young teenagers, but it is well worth any risk of discomfort. Be prepared; you and your students may be surprised by what comes out in this kind of writing. Occasionally, however, several of you may decide not to show it to anyone or read it aloud. Honor these decisions. You can decline; let them to decline.

GRADING STUDENTS' ORIGINAL POETRY

It works well to customize a rubric used in the past that outlines the knowledge and skills you are measuring as you read students' poetry. Is it their ability to write an original poem based on the following?

- length or number lines?
- use of specific kinds or number of poetic devices?
- a specific rhyme or rhythm pattern?
- fresh use of language: vivid verbs, concrete nouns?
- words chosen for their sound and expressive power?
- matching the pattern of a published poem?

Decide what a complete poem will be in terms of features as those mentioned earlier. What would a student need to demonstrate to earn a C, a B, or an A? Consider:

- C = poem meets minimum-length requirement and has three of five suggested poetic devices to recreate an experience or observation.
- B = poem meets minimum-length requirement, has all five suggested poetic devices, and has words that reveal an identifiable tone of the poet about the experience or observation.
- A = poem exceeds minimum-length requirement, has all five suggested poetic devices used in fresh and creative ways, reflects words that reveal an identifiable tone of the poet, and has active verbs and concrete nouns that clearly and cleverly recreate an identifiable experience or observation.

Then, ask students to write a note explaining how their original poem fits the definition of poetry given in your class or this one I use from an ordinary dictionary.

> Definition: Poetry is literature designed to convey a vivid and imaginative sense of experience, especially by the use of condensed language chosen for its sound and suggestive power as well as for its meaning and by the use of such literary devices as structured meter, natural cadences, rhyme, and metaphor.[4]

READING, RESPONDING, AND WRITING ABOUT POETRY—TELLING THE T.I.M.E.

Responding to poetry by writing an essay is an important component of poetry study. You can combine writing poetry and writing about poetry in the same unit. If so, it would be beneficial to begin with a quick review of Poetry T.I.M.E., as suggested in figure 7.1, that reminds students to consider a poem from multiple perspectives during multiple readings. Then select and project on the screen an appropriately challenging poem, and have the students conduct a T.I.M.E. analysis of it. Projecting the poem can be better for whole class work because all must focus their attention up front.

T.I.M.E. MNEMONIC

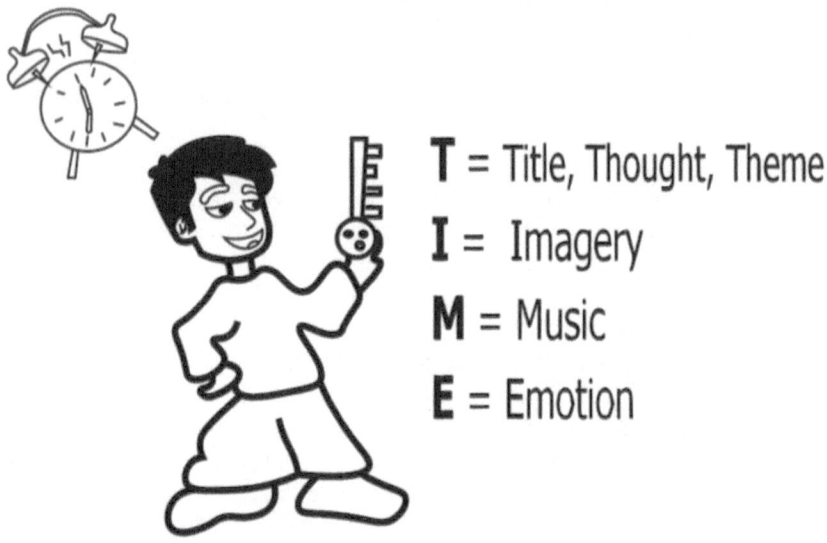

Figure 7.1.   T.I.M.E. is a key to understanding poetry
Source: Graphic by Nabeel Usmani

MULTIPLE READINGS HELP REVEAL MESSAGES

You can ask the students to read the poem silently before reading the poem aloud. Then invite a student to read the poem according to the punctuation, rather than just stopping at the end of each line. This second reading helps students focus on the fact that poems sometimes include punctuation that serves the same functions used in prose. Punctuation clarifies the meaning of words organized in a particular order.

It is still beneficial to have a third reading of the poem by another student, who, by this time, may have an idea of what the poet may be trying to express. This student may choose to emphasize different words or read at a different pace and thus offer a third level of understanding. Then have the whole class read the poem aloud in unison. By the fourth reading students begin noticing the elements of imagery and music, and they may also sense some emotion—either expressed by the author or experienced by themselves, as readers.

MARKING THE POEM HELPS STUDENTS SEE PATTERNS

If you provide students copies of the poem, also give them a couple colored pencils. Then, as you read aloud, have the students consider what strikes them they may have missed when they read the poem to themselves. On the next reading, encourage the students to underline appealing or thought-provoking words and phrases. Then exchange pencils for another color and mark what attracts them on this reading. It is fine to underline the same word or phrase in a second color. Finally, conclude this version of multiple readings by asking students to read aloud the words phrases they have underlined. If one student reads a line first, it is all right for another student to repeat it. It is likely that the repeated words and phrases reveal the theme or main ideas of the poem.

IN-CLASS WRITING ABOUT POETRY— USING THE T.I.M.E.

Here is an assignment that guides but does not constrain students as they analyze a poem before writing about it. Model this approach, and then have students work in pairs, or independently, on a different poem.

Carefully read the chosen poem noting structure, imagery, and meaning or message for you. Then write a complete essay in response to the poem that includes the following:

- Summary of the poem: what is it about?
- Structure of the poem: what poetic devices does the poet use?
- Personal response to the poem: what poetic devices help create this personal response?
- A thesis statement that indicates the kind of poem it is and your personal response.
- A body that explains ways the structure of the poem influences your response.
- Quotations that support your observations.

You may write on the poem and use the space below it for your notes.

For homework or during the next class meeting, assign the students to write a three-part essay in which they write the analysis of that poem or one of their own choosing. They should use the information they gathered while "telling the T.I.M.E." of the poem.

ASSIGNING A POETRY PROJECT OR NOTEBOOK

An effective way to reinforce the interests raised and skills developed during a poetry unit is to have the students assemble a poetry notebook. The collection should include poems students have read and enjoyed as well as poems they have written themselves. Decide how much time you have to devote to this project, and select activities that may be organized around one or more of the following topics:

- poems by a single poet
- poems written on a single theme (love, family, hobby, seasons, etc.)
- poems employing common poetic devices
- poems reflecting a specific culture or nationality

Do inform your students at the beginning of the poetry unit that they are to create this poetry notebook. They can be thinking about and setting aside poems throughout the weeks you spend on formal poetry study. Encourage students to use available digital devices and computers to search for, write, and save their poems. Some students may decide to use original drawings or create video, digital, or audio components for their poetry notebooks that can be shared live or online. Remind them to keep a record of their sources, including URL addresses and dates viewed.

COLLABORATING ACROSS THE CONTENT AREAS

The poetry project could be an effective interdisciplinary assignment. Teachers in different content areas could plan assignments due as a summative project at the end of April, a typical time the United States celebrates Poetry Month. In this case, the contents could be poems written about what students are studying in the courses of the cooperating teachers. Each teacher would read and grade the projects based on criteria established by those teachers. Consider each teacher being responsible for their course content and two other traits on a Six Traits rubrics.

INCORPORATE RESEARCH ABOUT POETS

Assigning a poetry project is a good way to incorporate a research component into your instruction, too. Your school librarian may help students find background and biographical information on their selected poet and, if access to the Internet is available, you may simply direct students to age-appropriate

Exchange poetry across the country by Internet

websites. If the option is right for your school setting, have students create an electronic version of this notebook and post it for sharing with other students across the country and around the world.

In your planning for the project, check online sites with safe environments for students to post their writing. Consider class anthologies using www.lulu.com, a free site for composing and for a modest fee includes an option to print booklets that others can purchase. Some sites require parent permission for younger students to post online.

The choices students must make for this project—conducting research, writing and selecting poems, deciding formats, creating order, using technology, collaborating with classmates—are all part of an authentic assessment where students are showing what they know and are able to do based on skills they bring and those they learn under your carefully designed tutelage.

CELEBRATING THEIR WRITING

By this time, you and your students have read, written, and performed poetry in class, and you are ready for a special poetry celebration. It can be simple—a special time during the regular class period or a bigger event to which family and friends are invited to meet in the cafeteria, auditorium, or library.

CELEBRATION DAY

- Have students display their notebooks laid on tables like a science fair exhibition.
- Invite guests to leave Post-it notes with commendations on poems they like.
- Have one student as master or mistress of ceremonies who welcomes the guests.
- Have a second master or mistress of ceremonies who calls on the volunteers to recite their poems.
- Invite everyone in attendance to share light refreshments.

Be prepared for on-the-spot volunteers, who see the joy of performing and want to share the spotlight.

All of this means planning well ahead to reserve the space, invite administrators, have microphones in place, and refreshments bought or brought and laid out. Students should be recruited to help set up and clean up.

If you work together with other teachers, you may be able to turn this into a school-wide event. Post student poetry in the halls. Write it with colored chalk on the sidewalks (with permission of the principal, of course). Encourage the students to enter their writing in local, state, and national poetry contests in print, audio-visual, or digital formats, or to perform in age-appropriate poetry slam venues.

WELCOME RECITATIONS IN HOME LANGUAGES

An end-of-unit poetry celebration is the perfect time to invite students to recite poetry of their nationality, culture, or home language. Since poetry is written to be heard, it does not matter whether everyone in the audience understands every spoken word. Just invite these students to recite a favorite poem, and let them bask in the pleasure of sharing themselves in a language close to their hearts. To enhance the experience of the listeners, though, encourage those students who are comfortable reciting the poem in a language other than English to first give a brief synopsis of the poem.

CONNECT BEYOND THE CLASSROOM

Many educator websites provide online opportunities for students to expand their knowledge of topics addressed in the books used in language arts courses across North America. For instance, a teacher whom I met from Florida and I, then a teacher in California, set up a "Coast to Coast" project in which students wrote to each other about the poetry that both classes were studying. We posted selected works by a poet from our own state and invited the students to discuss their responses online. The resulting conversations offered the students insightful peer perspectives while affirming that students on both coasts have to learn and apply the same kinds of analytical and evaluative skills during their study of poetry.

CONCLUSION

Poetry writing need not lead to student defeat or frustration, sending your school-year tour bus into a ditch. Your creative, well-structured lesson planning and nurturing instruction can create an environment in which students compose and recite poetry with pleasure and poise, with personality and pride. Their original poems are likely to become valued souvenirs of this portion of the trip. You can confirm the fine work of your students and encourage them to submit their poetry for publication in print or on safe Internet sites. Of course, support students who decide to enter local poetry slams and attend them if you can.

Celebrate poetry with your students, and watch as what they learn about the power of careful word choices, deliberate crafting, attention to organization, and impact of appearance carries over into their reading and writing other texts they study. With your help, providing them with a key and T.I.M.E. to unlock the poetry of others, and to release the poetic endowments of their own, your students look forward to "versing" their lives in poetry, the way I learned to turn my prose thoughts about my son, Robert, into the verse that opens this chapter.

NOTES

1. *Common Core Anchor Standards.* http://www.corestandards.org/ELA-Literacy/W/6// (accessed September 29, 2018).
2. Edward Lear. n.d. *Poem Hunter.* Accessed October 1, 2018. https://www.poemhunter.com/poem/there-was-an-old-man-in-a-tree/.
3. Joseph Epstein, "The Personal Essay: A Form of Discovery." In *The Norton Book of Personal Essays*, edited by Joseph Epstein (New York: W. W. Norton and Company, 1997), 15.
4. *Houghton-Mifflin College Dictionary.* 1986, s.v. "poetry."

Chapter 8

Entertain and Explore Life: Writing Short Stories

> Short stories should be written to entertain the reader.
>
> —Jeremy Hubble[1]

Storytelling is a fundamental activity in many families. The stories may be told to entertain, admonish, persuade, or simply to pass along the history and heritage of a culture. You may find that moving from listening to stories to reading and analyzing stories to writing stories of their own can be an empowering experience for students of all ages. They have stories to tell.

Inviting students to write their stories seems a natural way to reinforce academic skills while you encourage and affirm each student, personally. As they write about real or imagined experiences modeling the elements of fiction they already are learning, they inevitably develop better understanding of themselves and the world around them.

Students who learn the basic elements of narrative fiction often are better prepared to write well-structured stories of their own. As they read and discuss the work of their peers, you can listen to the features of the short story they mention to assess what they are coming to know and learning to do. Some students are eager to begin whether or not they understand the plot, point of view, and theme, but they may be equally eager to learn why their stories appeal to readers.

Including units for short story writing in your lessons offers several opportunities to learn about one another while fulfilling curriculum standards guiding most school English language arts programs. Those standards say that students should be able to "write narratives to develop real or imagined experiences or events using effective technique, well-chosen details, and well-structured event sequences."[2] The early drafts your students write using some of the ideas in this chapter should give you a good sense of specific elements of fiction to review along the way because the students are being encouraged to model what they have read. After experimenting with different ways to draft, invite them to flesh out their stories and submit them for evaluation and publication.

CHANNELING THE MASTERS

This term "to channel" used metaphorically simply means to consider the guidance of those who have come before that can provide a protective passage from one source to another. Edgar Allan Poe suggested that a short story should be written to be read in a single sitting and be so focused as to produce a unifying effect. To help your students focus their attention and to create a single impact in an entertaining way, consider having them work with a single protagonist in a limited setting who strives to resolve a single conflict. Also refer them regularly to storytellers they enjoy as well as the texts you have studied and viewed together.

BEWARE: BUMPS AHEAD

Since some students are not keen about this assignment, allot just enough time for all students to draft a brief story—not so long that you cannot maintain enthusiasm for the task. Be observant as you coach the students through this process and adjust the teaching pace as needed. Initially, plan to spend two to three weeks. Encourage students to experiment with strategies you suggest, but do not limit those who are moving along nicely without them.

The hint is to tell students that it might help them to tell the story to themselves, in their heads, before writing. If they can describe to themselves in a few sentences a story with a problem to be resolved, they probably have a story. Stress the ideas of conflict and resolution so they create stories that have real plots rather than just a series of incidents. You also could set up pairs of students and encourage the partners to tell each story to one another. Or suggest that students try their story out loud at home, or tell it to their seat partner on the bus or to friends at lunch table.

KEEPING IT PERSONAL
WITHOUT BEING INTRUSIVE

Experienced authors know that using personal experiences lends authenticity to their writing. But asking students to do this may cause resistance if they

Solicit student ideas for story

feel they are being asked to spill their guts, so it may be better to take it slow. Allow distance between what you require them to write based on their personal lives. You could suggest they put themselves into the "story" becoming a friend or foe of the person they write about or becoming the protagonist in the setting they may describe based on a painting or photograph as described in chapter 5 in the section called "Entering Art."

In other words, when assigning the narrative, move step by step from the impersonal to the personal, encouraging students to use their experiences to flesh out their narratives but not requiring them to describe their own specific experiences.

CREATING A CLASS STORY

Design a brief class lesson for which students create a basic plot outline:

- Ask for a protagonist.
- Ask for a setting (any setting!).
- Ask for a conflict likely involving an additional character.
- Ask how the conflict might be resolved.
- What attempts would the protagonist probably make to solve the problem?

- Who cares? This is toughest question but one that pushes students to create more interesting stories with some intrigue.
- Be visual: to help visual learners, diagram the plot on the board or screen as you create the story. See figure 8.1 for diagram of plot line.

In other words, do your best to ensure that students are thinking "story" before they begin writing their narratives. Let interested students draw their ideas, including plotlines and character "sketches," before they try to express those creative thoughts formally in another medium—in this case, the short story.

Two to three weeks is usually sufficient time for student story drafting. Students who are interested in pursuing this kind of writing should be encouraged to revise and polish their stories for submission to the school's literary magazine or online zines and contests. You could create a simple loose-leaf binder anthology and display it in the school library. If you decide to display student writing online or in the community library, be cautious about student privacy. Obtain parent permission to include first and last names of students below eighteen years.

CROSSING CURRICULUM BORDERS FOR WRITING INSPIRATION

Students generally value opportunities to use what they learn in one class to enhance the work they do in others. Why not invite your students to use

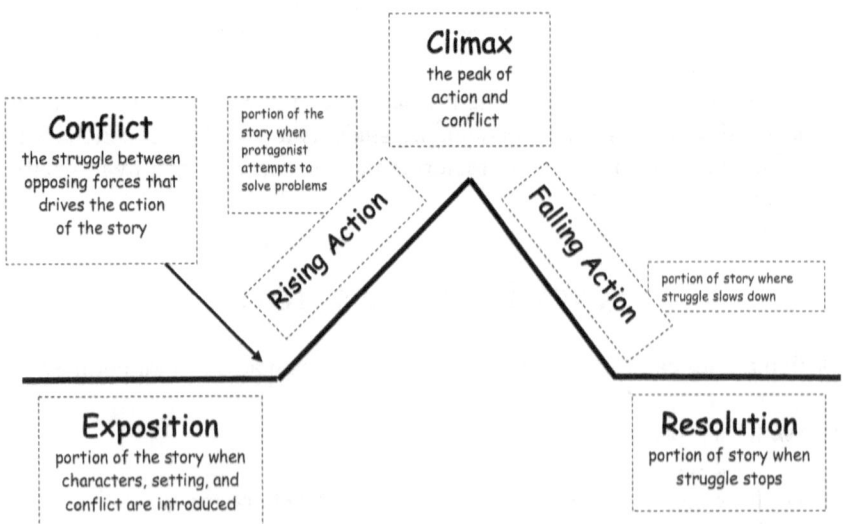

Figure 8.1. Plotline helps students structure of their short stories

people, places, and incidents from history, science, sports, or social studies as fodder for short story writing. You could even collaborate with your colleagues in other content areas to arrange one or two units to be developed concurrently or subsequently.

For example, after the students have studied a particularly rich historical period with lots of intriguing characters or action-filled adventures, invite students to write stories inspired by those people, places, and events. After all, there is an entire subgenre of historical fiction. After students have studied units in life science or physical science in which they have investigated concepts in biology, geology, chemistry, or physics, invite stories that incorporate that information. After all, there is an entire subgenre of science fiction.

Students can do the same kind of cross-curricular writing by incorporating their newly gained experiences in art and music, math, and physical education. The specific details about a piece of music or solving a math problem or rules in a sports game can make their story more entertaining and believable. After all, there is an entire subgenre of _____. You get it. Fiction writers utilize what they know about all kinds of subjects. Encourage your students to draw on their studies to enhance their short story writing.

HELPING "STORY-LESS" STUDENTS

Sometimes students still have difficulty coming up with a story to write. What to do?

1. Ask them to model a story they already have read for class but with characters and settings that are familiar to them. Following that pattern reminds them of the elements of fiction.
2. Consider a version of "Entering Art" during which students view a piece of art and pretend they are a part of the scene, the art reflects a dream a character is having, or the art is the setting for their story. Select art from the myriad websites with classical, contemporary, and modern art paintings and/or photos.
3. Then, invite students to expand this experience into a short story in which a specific character, in a specific place—could be based on the painting—attempts at least three different ways to resolve a single conflict.
4. Have students bring to class pictures from print or online publications and then write stories to accompany these images. For example, a week before beginning the story writing assignment, assign students to bring in three pictures—one of each that meets the following criteria:

- only one person in the picture
- a group of people in a specific place
- scenery only—a place, with no people

You should discourage the students from choosing pictures of easily identifiable persons, such as sports figures, film, or music stars, to reduce the temptation for the students to limit their imaginations, and have their story characters become exactly like celebrity personae.

Organize and store the pictures in three labeled envelopes until it is time to start the story writing a few days later. It is good for students to forget about the article, magazine, or setting from which they took the pictures, so ask them to bring in the pictures about a week before you plan to use them. This break allows time for those who may not have access to magazines at home to come before or after school to search through the box of magazines you may keep in your room or for students to print out pictures from a neighborhood library or school computer.

SET UP PREWRITING ASSIGNMENT BASED ON PICTURES

1. Before the class arrives for a day of story writing, prepare with prompts on handout, on a poster, or projected on electronic slides.
2. Arrange the pictures in the three categories, face down on a desk or tabletop.
3. Ask students to prepare with paper and a pen or pencil on their desks, or their computers opened to a blank page in a Word-processing program.
4. Invite them to come forward to take one picture from each pile before returning to their seats. You might even play a lyric-free song and have students march up to the music, pick up the three pictures, and return to their seats before the tune concludes. Yes, there may be clowning around. But as long as students are orderly, ignore it.
5. Give students two minutes to look at the pictures they have and decide which one they would like to write about. They can return the rejects so others can use them. Complete the selection in seven minutes or so. Then urge students to keep what they have and see what happens. Few students fail to come up with a workable story.
6. Set a timer for five minutes for a quick write—nonstop writing until the timer goes off.
7. Encourage students to write as though their chosen picture illustrates the story they are drafting.
8. Suggest that they begin writing either in the first person as a character in the story or as an omniscient writer who reveals the thoughts and feelings of the characters. Remind them of the details in figure 8.2 showing points of view.

Entertain and Explore Life   113

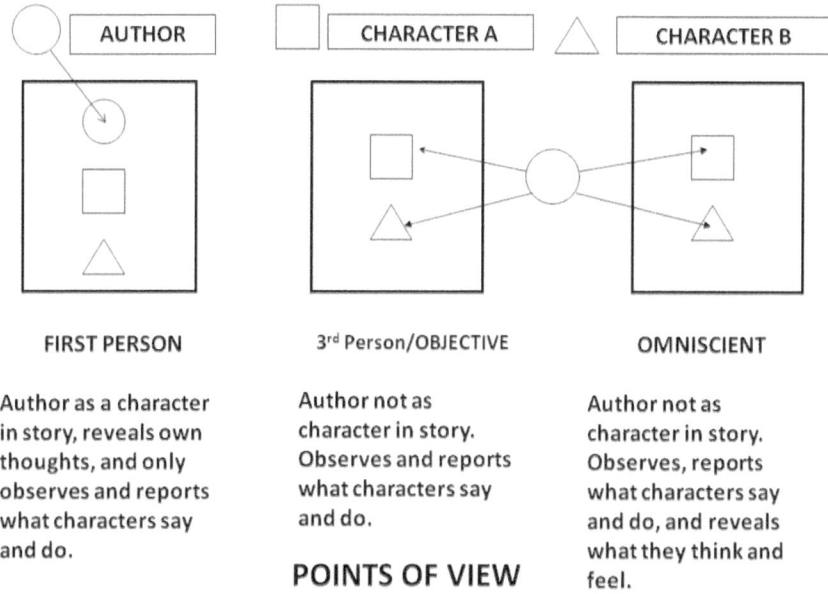

POINTS OF VIEW
Diagram adapted from work of Blair and Gerber, 1959

Figure 8.2.

9. If students cannot think immediately of what to write, direct their attention to the posted instructions or distribute a handout with the following prompts:

   If using the picture with one person, write as though you are that person. Write about

   - why you are in this place,
   - what happened just before the picture was taken, and
   - what's on your mind.

   If using the picture of a group of people, choose one of the people and write in that persona. Talk about

   - why you are here with this person/these people,
   - how you feel about the others, and
   - what happened just before the picture was taken.

If using the scenic picture of a place, make this the setting of the story and describe it using such strong, vivid images that an artist could draw the scene using just your writing. Reveal

- the time period (day, season, historical period),
- what happened just before the picture was taken, and
- what is going to happen in this place.

When the timer goes off, invite the students to reread their draft and circle any ideas that might be developed into a story which has characters in a specific place, confronted with and attempting to overcome some specific conflict. Remind them that short stories usually take place in a short period of time, often within a single hour, day, or week. Give your authors-to-be the remainder of the period to expand on the ideas evoked by this quick write.

DESIGN MINI-LESSONS RELATING TO CONFLICT AND CHARACTER DEVELOPMENT

As the students continue writing in the coming days, encourage them to include at least three increasingly difficult obstacles to overcome. Remind them that in a successful story the protagonist solves the problem in a logical way or decides that there is no solution and after valiant attempts to solve the problem ceases the struggle. Discourage, "and then he woke up." Push them to consider alternatives that lead to a thoughtful, insightful, and even surprising but satisfying conclusion. Refer them to the plotline or narrative arc diagram they created while reading short stories.

By this time, most students are excited about developing their stories, so you can assign them to continue drafting their story for homework or to leave their quick write and notes in folders so they can resume writing the next class meeting. In the interim, encourage them to listen to the rhythm of conversations to attune their ears to writing realistic dialogue. You should not be surprised when many students return the next class meeting brimming with ideas of how to continue their story.

FLESHING OUT FLAT OR SKELETAL CHARACTERS

Use direct and indirect characterization. If students need reminders, refer them to characters in readings that they have already studied, paying attention to the way the authors revealed the characters' personality and motivation. As with fan fiction, modeling a favorite author can effectively jump-start students' writing. Remember the annual Hemingway imitation contests?

BUILDING SUSPENSE

Ask students to:

- circle the sentence in their story that indicates the conflict the protagonist is facing. No such sentence? Time to add one!;
- put a rectangle around the sentence in the story that identifies the antagonist; and
- draw a plotline of their story to verify that their protagonist is faced with a believable problem and is making logical choices while facing increasingly complicated obstacles to resolve the conflict. Remind them of the image of a roller-coaster ride.

Encourage students to revise so that their stories flow to a suspenseful climax. They should include the thoughts of the protagonist as he or she considers the final step to solving the problem. That final attempt before the climax often is an internal conflict during which the protagonist struggles with issues of right and wrong, safe and unsafe, advantageous and disadvantageous. Remind them that dialogue can reveal inner thoughts when one is writing in objective or third-person point of view. Remind them to refer to their notes on kinds of conflict as show in figure 8.3.

Complete the draft for homework. Assign students to bring a Word-processed copy for class in two days. If this homework assignment is not a

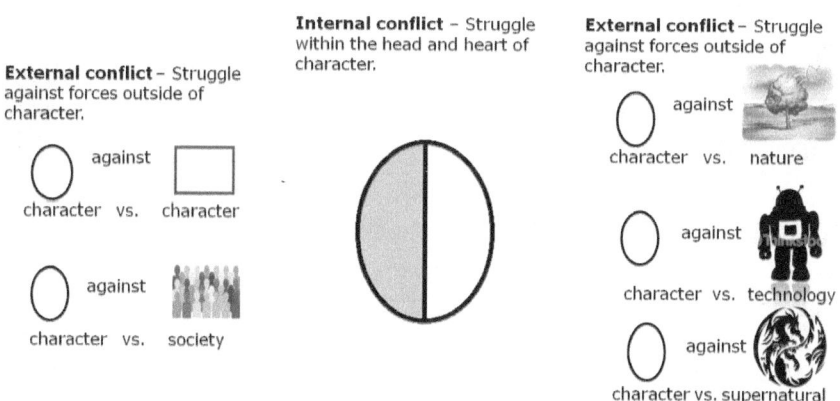

Figure 8.3. Internal/external conflict

realistic expectation for your students, arrange time to use the school computers for a couple of class periods. Encourage students to use the rubric the class creates or that you provide to evaluate the draft of their own story before submitting it for peer review.

UTILIZE PEER RESPONSES TO SUPPORT WRITERS

Now is the time for students to serve one another as helpful, encouraging peer responders. Establish either writer-responder partners or small (three or four students) writers' groups within the class. The partners or groups can review each other's drafts and make suggestions. The purpose is to give positive and constructive feedback in tune with the basic rubrics the students have already created. Positive: "What a vivid descriptive passage. I can almost feel the wind blowing across the meadow." Encouraging suggestions: "Wow, have you thought about telling what the character is thinking right here?" Professional writers frequently have brittle egos. So do amateur writers of any age.

Students usually have good ideas for improving stories. However, to keep the peer comments on track, provide the criteria they are to consider on a printed peer-response sheet with a rubric that includes statements about content and creativity, organization and flow, and quality of vocabulary and correctness relating to mechanics, usage, and grammar. Your budding authors then can share the assessment standards and presumably the stories with parents or guardians, too. A number of teacher websites, such as Rubistar, have templates and programs for creating and modifying rubrics to meet the specific requirements of a variety of language arts assignments.

Once the students understand the rubric, let them have a go at it. Provided you have given the writers enough time and in-class mini-lessons to do their own revisions first, the peer review process should go smoothly and helpfully. Here are two ways to conduct either the partner (or small group) or workshop responding sessions.

Option A: Working in Pairs—Desk-Touching Exercises

Ask students to pull desks together to work in pairs. Touching desks suggests sharing a common work surface, physical permission to collaborate. Or if your room is furnished with tables, you may have students pull their chairs together so that the conversation between two students can be private, without distracting or disturbing their other tablemates. The rest is gloriously simple but effective:

- Remind students to speak in six-inch voices so only their partners can hear them as each one reads his or her story to the other. Let the partner hear how the story sounds as narrated by the author. If there is an odd number of students, serve as a partner yourself using the story you have been drafting along with the class.
- Encourage students to listen for consistency in point of view and verb tense.
- Then, as students respond to authors, let the authors take a few notes on their own drafts.
- Once the comments are concluded, allow time in class for authors to begin making corrections and revisions as they see fit. Assure them that their stories are their own works; they do not have to make the suggested revisions. But they do need to address grammatical issues and should correct other problems that may cloud communication.

Sometimes it is necessary to modify your teaching timeline based on what you overhear during the desk-touching exercises. If the majority of the students sound as though they need another day of writing before sharing in groups, extend the due date. Keep students on task by making your presence felt and coaching their understanding as needed.

Option B: Working in Groups—Writers' Workshop

Adapt the RAG format described in chapter 2. Before the final draft is due, take the time to review the grading rubric with the students so they can once again assess their own work before you grade it. If they notice something that should be corrected, ask them to do so neatly. You want to see what they know, not a photo-ready version of the story. When students have a clear idea of what is expected of them, they are more likely to meet those expectations—the fewer surprises, the fewer challenges to grades.

You may decide to schedule a second read-around session when the students have finished their stories and are ready to submit them for publication outside the school. In this case, if this has been a generally positive and supportive group of students, you could ask them to rank and rate the stories of their peers. If so, you may find it useful to use the story evaluation chart, shown in figure 8.4, as a guide to set up an assignment, which suggests that students work with papers without names on them and from a different class period. This gives students a little more anonymity and makes for more objective reading.

Manuscript #		1	2	3	4	5
Criteria						
Characters	flat, round, dynamic					
Characterization	direct, indirect					
Conflict	unclear, typical, compelling					
Rising Action	single or multiple attempts to solve					
Resolution	anticipated, believable, surprising, but logical					
Setting	sight, sound, taste, touch, smell					
Dialogue	stiff, believable, realistic					
Mechanics, Usage, Grammar	not, somewhat, very distracting					
Vocabulary	flat, adequate, vivid					
	OVERALL RATING (1-5)					

Figure 8.4. Use chart to have students rank and rate stories anonymously

GRADING DURING STORY COMPOSITION

Monitor student work but resist the temptation to grade it based on final content criteria. Each day you expect the students to come prepared with work on their stories, consider rubber-stamping the last page written and record check in your grade book to indicate that the students are completing the drafting assignments. If they are working on computers, they should post a copy in the class folder set up for them to post into, but one from which they can open and read or delete. You can then view them before, during, or after class and get an idea of how stories are coming along. You can also post a general commendation or recommendation. Do not feel obligated to post daily, or students will begin to expect them. They should go first to classmates in their group.

It really is too early to begin evaluating the quality of their work. Why? Because these early drafts are like practice sessions or training drills. For sports, it is the scores of the games that go in the record book to determine the success of the season. However, coaches do keep records of attendance and make remarks during practices. You can, too.

Consider this grading guideline to show the value of prewriting and peer feedback.

- 30 points—full credit for draft finished on time
- 15 points for constructive feedback (five points for each of three classmates' draft)
- 45 points for final draft (graded on scale using customized rubric)
- 10 points—full credit for self-reflection turned in on time

Keep observation notes as students write and respond to peers

MODEL AS YOU TEACH

Now is the time to serve as the students' model and coach. Your attitude is important, and it is more empathetic if you draft a story yourself as the students are drafting theirs and offer yours for comments, too. Model making appropriate journal comments or suggestions, offering positive statements even as you point out a weakness that needs to be addressed: "Great idea for a setting." "Do you think you have enough conflict?" "Is that enough description of the protagonist so that readers could get to know her better?" "This section suddenly changes the story's point of view. Do you want to stay with first person so the reader doesn't get confused?"

Whenever you respond to students' creative work orally or in writing, you run the risk of unintentionally deflating their enthusiasm. Often you can get at story problems simply by asking questions. If a student needs more direction than what you can provide with general questions, try more directive questions: "What do you think about rewriting the scene so it seems more realistic—something that might actually happen?" "How do you think adding some thought shots that tell or show what characters are thinking can increase the suspense?"

Recording daily check marks in your grade book provides support for student progress, letting them know that writing is a process and that drafting is a step that counts. If, during this drafting period, you have to report to parents or an administrator about students' performance, you can rely on the comments you have made in the journals along with any other notes you make about students' active involvement in the daily assignments.

GUIDES FOR STUDENT FINAL DRAFTS

- Print final drafts double-spaced on white paper with one-inch margins, using ten- or twelve-point font. Times New Roman, Arial, and Bookman are most readable (avoid unusual fonts).
- Final story should be three to five pages long.
- Add a title sheet with story title with no quotation marks, student's full name, the class and time period it meets, the teacher's name (spelled correctly), and the due date, arranged neatly on the page.
- Use the picture from the first classroom exercise as an illustration with final draft, if desired. Or include an original drawing or a computer-generated image. Be sure to give credit if using an image from a website. (Write the web address in small letters under the image. See Insert CAPTION option in computer program.)

Students can provide useful feedback to classmates

- Submit all work on the story, stapled together. Include a handwritten note on the bottom for each section: Draft 1, Peer Response; Draft 2, First Plotline; Final Draft; and any others that show evidence of the process. The packet is visible and tactile evidence of what it takes to write a good story. If students are submitting stories online, earlier drafts still can be included in final file, by saving each day's work as a separate file that includes the date.
- Include one-paragraph self-reflection and grade earned using grading rubric for this assignment.
  "I earned _____ on this assignment because_____."
- Celebrate! When all of this work is organized and stapled together for submission with title page, or saved and sent, do something fun.

CELEBRATE STUDENT WRITING WITH AUTHORS' READING

Do follow through with a full-class celebration—like an authors' reception or a book-publishing party in class. Invite students to bring in "neat-to-eat" treats. (Be cautious about treats with nuts to which some students have severe allergic reactions. Cold water is a lovely beverage, especially if you add slices of lemon and serve in small paper cups with decorations on them; and water doesn't stain if spilled!) You might randomly select stories to read aloud to the class yourself or invite the authors to read—as dramatically as they would like to do. Let the authors embellish their reading if they are comfortable. Join the fun by reading something that you have written.

PLAN AHEAD TO PUBLISH STUDENT WRITING

The final-final step for some students might be publishing their story on campus—in print form, in digital form on your pages of the school website, in an off-campus printed periodical, or on one of the websites that publish student work. Carefully choose from the myriad sites now available on the Internet. Avoid those with inappropriate advertising and those that do not provide for privacy of students' personal information.

Consider collaborating with other teachers in your school and planning a school anthology to publish by the end of the school year. Offering students a few points of extra credit is enough for simply submitting their work to an out-of-school publication. It is a big step for some of your emerging writers.

And do not be the least surprised when one or two students who submit their work each year have it selected for a print journal or anthology. This simply encourages others to try the next time.

Your librarian may agree to display in the library a loose-leaf binder with the stories your students write. Just get one of those white binders with a clear pocket cover and slip in a student-designed or computer-generated cover, and with a table of contents of the stories arranged alphabetically by author. Students who view the collection are not likely to mark or deface the book; students tend to respect peers' work and enjoy reading it, especially the older students who remember when their writing was similarly displayed. Or you can publish using one of the online sites on which you can create an electronic literary magazine.

CONCLUSION

Just do it. Go ahead and allot class time to write and then offer students an opportunity to publish their own stories locally in your classroom or library. Consider going public in a printed periodical or digital magazine All this will validate that what your budding authors have to say is important enough to revise and edit, to polish and share with others These publications will be like photo albums of your journey with your fellow travelers, working together to meet the curriculum targets or state course standards for English language arts.

NOTES

1. Jeremy Hubble, "Here We Are Now, Entertain Us: Poe's Contributions to the Short Story." *Jeremy Hubble.* April 7, 1996. http://geocities.jeremyhubble.com/poe.html (accessed June 29, 2018).
2. "English Language Arts Standards 'Anchor Standards' College and Career Readiness Anchor Standards for Language." *Common Core State Standards Initiative.* 2011. http://www.corestandards.org/ (accessed June 29, 2018).

Chapter 9

Dramatize It Write: Reviewing Drama and Drafting One-Act Plays

> I order you to be silent! And I issue a collective challenge! Come, I'll write down your names. Step forward, young heroes! You'll all have a turn; I'll give each of you a number. Now, who wants to be at the top of the list? You, sir? No? You? No? [Silence] No names? No hands. . . . Then I'll get on with my business.
>
> —Cyrano speaking in *Cyrano de Bergerac*, by Edmond Rostand[1]

Cyrano's rousing speech may not have been as successful as he would have liked, but he certainly delivered it with enthusiasm and passion. You need the same passion to draw your students into reading and writing drama. In this chapter are techniques that can produce a far better response than poor Cyrano elicited.

Drama permeates teachers' and students' lives via television, movies, school productions, YouTube, and so many other venues. This pervasiveness makes it a challenge to teach dramatic literature simply by reading or writing drama without acting it. But that is just the way some drama is handled in English classes. That need not be said of yours.

Drama, like other narrative literature, is written to tell a story of characters facing conflict. In this genre, dramatists create their narratives to be performed by actors who assume the roles of characters in the story. In drama, however, the setting—the time and place—is revealed primarily through sets, lights, props, and costumes, and readers must rely more heavily on the dialogue that reveals character and advances plot.

Unfortunately, inexperienced students are tempted to skip those important stage directions; such readers tend to jump directly to the dialogue. They become confused, even frustrated when they do not understand what is really happening. Consequently, the aspects of drama to teach first are its unique features. Begin the unit by pointing out those distinctive elements as you remind your maturing writers that characters and conflict are common to fiction, in general. But do not waste valuable time analyzing the writing until you and the class have completed the first reading. Add writing drama after reading and acting out drama.

REVIEW LITERARY DEVICES AND VOCABULARY FOR DRAMA

During class while studying a play is an excellent time to expand or reinforce the list of literary elements of fiction and poetry. When you assign students to write their own short dramas, they will have more precise language to talk about it with one another. You may encourage or even require students to experiment and include a minimum number of techniques in their own short drama for this course. For example, as you study *Cyrano de Bergerac*, this list could include those elements that Rostand used so brilliantly, such as

- allusion,
- ballad,
- dramatic irony,
- mood, and
- verbal irony.

Plan carefully for happy, not sad, experience teaching playwriting
Source: Sudowoodo

If the play is in your anthology, you may rely on the literary terms and vocabulary featured in the text. The editorial staff usually does a fine job of selecting words students need to know to understand the play, along with some that would be good for them to add to their speaking and writing vocabularies. Of course, take time for students to look up and talk about any other words that interest them or trip them up when they are reading or discussing the play you have chosen. By the second semester when many course outlines suggest teaching drama, the students are comfortable with each other and with you, are open to acknowledging gaps in their understanding, and are accustomed to looking up words they do not know.

GETTING INTO THE PLAY

The best preparation for writing a play is a good, in-class experience with a play. Start with the list of characters, the author's description of setting, and the stage directions. Encourage students to predict. For example, if there are family members, ask the students what conflicts they anticipate among those persons considering their age and gender. Think about the setting. What is

Creating tableaux helps imagine action in drama

likely to occur in the time and place the author has chosen? Based on the stage directions, where should the characters be positioned when the curtain opens?

If the students have previously studied the elements of fiction, they anticipate from these opening observations and even predict that the play will follow the now-familiar plotline with exposition, rising action, climax, falling action, and resolution.

STAGING TABLEAUX

To help students get a feel for drama, ask them to read the opening scene silently. Then, with no explanation from you of what they have read, invite one student to come silently to the front of the class and stand where a specific character would stand if he or she were on stage. Then, one at a time, beckon other students individually to assume the persona of characters and to take their places in relation to those already positioned there in the front. Ask the rest of the class to observe silently until all the scene's characters are positioned. At that time, call for a freeze to create a tableau, montage, or representation of that scene.

Now ask the class its opinions of the character placement. Before those in the tableau lose their concentration and begin squirming or melting, unfreeze them so they can return to their seats to join the discussion. Invite participants from the tableau to identify lines from the play that support their own choice of position.

Other students can look at the text of the play to determine the passages that justify the tableau just presented or to propose an arrangement more accurate to the text. Of course, those who disagree should be asked to quote from the text to show why an alternate placement seems more accurate. Taking time to consider placement on the stage will help your students write more realistic drama when they begin their own scripts.

Your well-taught students know to pay attention to what happens in the opening sections of any work of fiction, whether short story, narrative poetry, or novel. As they continue reading the play on their own, they are able to follow the plotline and to answer in their journals such questions as the following:

- *Who* are the protagonist and antagonist(s)?
- *What* is the conflict?
- *When* does the main action occur?
- *Where* does the main action take place (other than onstage)?

- *Why* do characters act the way they do?
- *How* does the writer have the characters solve the problems raised in the play?

Assigning this exploratory writing activity about the opening act focuses students' attention on the main characters as they are being introduced. It also focuses them on the conflicts which play writers reveal early in the exposition of their works. Yes, the script lists the names in the cast of characters; some dramatists even mention the relationship among the characters, but the reader/viewer usually does not know the personality or motivations of these characters until the play begins. Since you want your students to be able to follow the play without having to go back too often to figure out who's who and what's what, assign this Five Ws and H journal entry right away.

TAKING NOTES WHILE READING

While a quick read is usually best for overall narrative comprehension, many film-oriented students have difficulty tracking characters because they cannot see them. These students may benefit from a simple graphic organizer. If your students are not permitted to write in their books, ask the students to keep character-related notes in their reading journal. They can make three columns:

Column one: character name
Column two: character traits (use words and/or sketches)
Column three: page number (act and scene)

These notes and drawings can prepare students to participate actively in discussions about ways the playwrights unveil the personalities and motivations of the characters. Writing and graphically representing these facts and impressions slow the readers, and they pay attention to the crucial information the dramatist reveals in the opening scenes, thus reducing confusion and frustration later.

Once these details are firm in their minds, students can read more confidently and understand more deeply. Nevertheless, you probably have to remind your students that reading a play is different from watching one. As readers, they must use all the clues the author gives in the dialogue and in the stage directions to imagine what the characters look like and what movements they may be making onstage. Some may find sketching and diagraming what they visualize stretches their thinking and helps them see the play as they read it and when they write their own.

COMPARING AND CONTRASTING FILM VERSIONS OF PLAYS

When you study *Cyrano de Bergerac*, for example, you could show video clips from both an English version of the play and French version of the play starring Gerard Depardieu. The French version can be advantageous even if students don't speak that language; students can pay attention to the action that is implied by the dialogue they've been reading. The fact that this version is performed "in the field" and "on location" and not onstage provides an opportunity to discuss how stage and screen communicate differently—especially with lighting, close-ups, scene transitions, and audio/sound. This lesson may give students ideas about lighting and sound instructions to include when they flesh out the scripts of their own plays.

Next ask students to discuss or write about the differences they note between the two media. Some students are disappointed because they have imagined the people, places, and scenes to be different from what is shown in the video. This gives an opening to talk about the power of language to create images in our minds and the pleasure of reading widely and independently.

The key for you is to decide why the video clips are being shown and to determine whether they help or hurt students to reach the standards for reading, viewing, and critical thinking laid out for the course. Sometimes these lessons will prepare for lessons on reading and writing for visual media. Sometimes more is just too much.

DEEPENING UNDERSTANDING OF LITERARY DEVICES

By the second semester, your students are at ease identifying, discussing, and writing about most literary devices except theme and irony. Therefore, when you plan lessons for drama study, design activities to help them develop greater confidence with these features of literature. You could quiz them with quotations from the play and ask students to identify the speaker, the situation, and the importance of that speech to characterization, plot advancement, or setting. These informal assessments measure their retention of this knowledge.

To understand and identify literary themes in plays, students must understand the plotline. They may find it useful first to refer to their one-paragraph summaries of the Five Ws and H questions. Just as you taught during the short story unit, ask the students to write thematic statements in which they identify the universal situation based on the conflict and the universal response to the situation based on the character's response to the conflict.

Inviting classmates to write a theme statement for drafts of their peer's play helps confirm to writers they are getting their point across.

It may help them write these theme statements by reminding them of what they learned in the short story unit. For those who need it, provide a sample formatted sentence with missing words:

When people _____ [the students fill in the situation], they _____ [the students fill in the response to the situation].

For one homework assignment, ask students to try writing some of these sentences in their reading journals. After students write the theme statements, they can later convert the SWBST (Somebody Wanted But So Then) phrases they may have learned in elementary school into simple sentences that generalize the concept captured in their preliminary drafts. Students soon recognize the universal quality of plays in much the way they saw them in other literary works studied this school year.

CRITIQUING A PLAY

Inviting students to use their analytical skills to evaluate a play is another effective way to write about reading. Students can use the nine yardsticks of value described in chapter 6 to write about a play the class has just studied or about a staged play the class views together.

READY TO WRITE A ONE-ACT PLAY

After studying a play, you may assign students to write one of their own and wonder where to begin. Reminding them that one key feature of drama is the dialogue reveals character and advances plot. Your students probably will be most challenged by what to have the actors doing while they are speaking. Cresence Birder, a teacher of ninth-grade students, addressed this with diagramming. She found that some students visualize better when they draw a diagram of the set or create charts with arrows, boxes, and circles. Periodically, invite your young students to share with their classmates the strategies they devise themselves to help them make sense of the text. Shared peer perceptions increase peer comprehension.

One student mentioned that blocking the scenes in plays helped her envision each scene, thus seeing more ways to have dialogue suggest action in the play. For many students, including this type of activity in the brainstorming process dynamically shaped the idea in their heads of the plot to fit the stage for which they were writing. Drawing some of the more significant moments of blocking helped to reveal what ideas were most realistic and doable in a theater space and which ideas would be far-fetched or perhaps better suited for film. Diagraming options motivate students to process their thoughts visually. This strategy may work for your students, too.

CONSIDER CROSS-CURRICULAR COLLABORATIONS

Students learn well when they see a link to other topics or subjects they are studying in other classes. Collaborating teachers who take time to create such lessons tend to have more success in getting their students to engage. One activity that lends itself well to cross-curricular collaboration is playwriting. Think about working with a colleague in history, science, art, or even music. Planning ahead and together can enhance everyone's experiences.

For example, in many schools eighth graders study physical science, which includes units on geology, weather, and the planets. Some eighth-grade literature lists include legends and myths. What a wonderful opportunity to write plays based on those myths that attempt to explain early man's rationale for the way the earth is formed, what causes weather, how stars come to be arranged in certain patterns, and why the planets exist.

Collaborating within and across departments enhances instruction

The same kind of teaming could work with colleagues in the history or social studies department. The students could write plays about historical people and events. Invite a teacher in the other department to work with you to design a joint assignment for which your students write a play set in the same historical period or that features the real people the students may be studying in one of those other classes. Students can incorporate the references to art and music of the period to support the authenticity, mood, or tone of their drama.

You teachers can share the grading. Consider using the features of the familiar Six Traits rubric or one that teachers from both departments create together. For example, one of you could read the student-written plays for accuracy of facts and ideas and for voice and sentence fluency. The other could read for organization, word choice, and conventions of drama writing as well as for mechanics, usage, and grammar. Such sharing halves the labor and doubles the pleasure, enhancing authenticity of assessment in both areas of study.

Or, after studying a group of short stories, you may decide to introduce students to playwriting instead of short story writing. Small groups could choose different short stories already studied and then create a group script based on one of the short stories and incorporate the elements of drama they learn in this drama unit based on notes given here taken from a Playwrights' Project teacher workshop.[2] Use questions as those that follow to have students self-check their progress in playwriting on the topic you assign or they choose.

PLAYWRITING CHECK-UP LIST

- *Who* are the two or three main characters in your play?
- *What* myth, short story, real person, or historical incident is the basis for your play?
- *What* do you want the audience to think, feel, and know as a result of reading or seeing your play?
- *When* does your play take place?
- *Where* does your play take place?
  - simple set and props requirements?
  - simple lighting required?
- *Why* are the characters in conflict (universal issue)?
  - parent child disagreement?
  - sibling rivalry?
  - desire for power or glory?

- peer pressure?
- boy meets girl?
- love triangle?

- *How* well does your play follow the guidelines for an effective drama script?

These also are questions students could consider about peer drafts during RAGs or in-class peer feedback created from this list:

- Is the plot focused on a single problem to be solved within a brief period of time?
- Is the personality of characters revealed primarily in dialogue; secondarily in action? (In other words, would a blind person be able to follow the flow of the story?)
- Does the dialogue introduce conflict early in the play?
- Does the dialogue sound like real conversation—brief, overlapping speeches and some fragments? (Here is a place for using local jargon, slang, and idioms.)
- Does the play have an identifiable beginning, middle, and end?
- Does the rising action include three increasingly more challenging obstacles in solving the problem?
- Is the climax realistic but not given away too soon?
- Does the resolution make sense based on the personality of characters?

A few more sophisticated questions to have students look for in later drafts include these:

- Do you avoid the use of narrator and let characters reveal themselves through dialogue?
- Do your minor characters serve as foils and help reveal personality of the protagonist?
- Do you include suggestions for lighting, sets, and props but allow dialogue to guide the director in his or her choices?

Depending on your students, assign each to author his or her own personal play or assign them to work as a group. By the second semester, when you may decide to teach playwriting, you have a better feel for what works best for your classes. If possible, arrange for a final performance of the best two or three plays your students write. This may be a practiced reading performed for other classes or in a full performance in your theater space for an invited audience of families and friends.

If you begin planning early enough in the first semester, your drama teacher may have time to join forces with you and plan time for the drama

Writing plays as a group can work

classes in the second semester to perform selected dramas of your budding dramatists. You can imagine how gratifying it would for these new playwrights to see their words come to life! And knowing their work is to be seen by their peers, families, and/or friends encourages the students to do a better job on the assignment. Win. Win. Win.

GRADING DURING PLAYWRITING

During the preliminary stages of playwriting, just give credit for completing each step, making note of participation instead of giving letters or percentages. It works better to keep students focused on process rather than grades, so any student who completes the step in the assignment on time should receive full credit. For example, a project worth 100 points could have subdivisions worth:

- 10 points for the plan for the play (answering questions on checklist provided earlier),
- 30 points for first draft,
- 20 points for first revision, and up to

- 40 points for the final script (based on rubric for final draft, given with assignment), and
- 10 points for self-reflection ("I contributed … to this project and earned this grade____").

Although students who do not complete a preliminary step receive no credit for that step, encourage them to participate fully in each group meeting and earn partial credit. Their contributions can enhance the final script, and they are likely to stay involved knowing they have not lost all by missing one assignment.

OBSERVING WORK SESSIONS: NO-STRESS ASSESSMENTS

As the students work together, use the opportunity to add to your notes about their behavior and contributions. You may have photocopies of seating charts on which to record these comments. Or have student names printed on large address labels to remind you to make notes for each of the students by the time the group playwriting meetings are finished. If you do not maintain individual student record sheets, you still can keep these notes in a folder to consult when needed. Your documenting student learning with these anecdotal assessments helps you to plan subsequent lessons and to prepare reports to parents or administrators should the need arise.

At the end of such a group project, have students evaluate their own contribution to the task. It is not necessary to ask them to comment on what others have done. Everyone in the group already knows if each has been supportive and cooperative, so you do not want to create situations for them to tattle. You want to avoid creating schisms among classmates, ones that damage the fragile egos of students of any age, even those who hide them with bluster.

SUMMATIVE ASSESSMENTS

At the end of the unit, you need to assess student learning by having students demonstrate their understanding of relationships among the characters, or the author's use of literary devices and the newly taught elements of drama of the play you study together. You could include options for which they can choose to

- summarize their learning by writing a poem about the play (see chapter 7 for pantoum poems);

- write an additional scene showing what happens next with characters who have survived;
- write a one-act play with the same conflict set in a contemporary time or different place;
- take a test;
- write a paper critiquing another play;
- produce a video with live performers; or
- create an animated video to post on your class website.

Among other plays that may work better for you are *A Doll's House* by Henrik Ibsen, *A Raisin in the Sun* by Lorraine Hansberry, *Bull Run* by Paul Fleischman, *The Mousetrap* by Agatha Christie, *The Monsters Are Due on Maple Street* by Rod Serling, *These Shoes of Mine* by Gary Soto, *Trifles* by Susan Glaspell, or *Witness* by Karen Hesse. Choose based on the cultural relevance of the students you teach that could be a window or mirror as well as pattern for writing their own play.

CONCLUSION

The study of drama can be an enriching experience for students and teachers because it incorporates six language arts skills: reading, writing, speaking, listening, representing, viewing and using technology, and a reason to practice cooperative learning. Moreover, while reading and writing drama students see how earlier-learned literary concepts are used in another genre of literature. Finally, drama is just fun because it appeals to a wide range of students across the range of multiple intelligences, especially those who like to talk, to watch, to move, and to act up. Who's left?

NOTES

1. Edmond Rostand, *Cyrano de Bergerac*, trans. Lowell Blair, *World Literature* (Lake Forest, Il.: Glencoe Macmillan/McGraw-Hill, 1991), 472.
2. You may wish to see the website accompanying this book to see my 1999 *California English* article "An Audience of One's Peers" based on workshop with the Playwrights Project (San Diego).

Chapter 10

Write for Public Speaking and Media

> The mark of an effective speaker is "the ability to adapt to a variety of audiences and settings and to perform appropriately in diverse social situations."
>
> —Clella Jaffe[1]

A dear friend is an accomplished welder and a talented musician, who can skillfully navigate a luxury tour bus through dense urban traffic and parallel park it with only inches to spare. And she is pathological about talking in public, except in casual conversation. She believes people judge her intellect by her speech;

Given her accented regional dialect and limited experience reading and writing regularly, she doesn't want to appear ignorant, so she self-muzzles. She seldom writes anything formal and writes only an informal note in an emergency. She owns a computer but seldom uses it. She believes people generally judge her education by her writing. Therefore, she corrals her speaking and writing, keeping herself to herself. Ask *her* to give a speech?

True, my friend left school early, married young, and soon became the sole wage earner for her family of three children. Even though she is gifted mentally and manually, she still feels hampered, unable to advance on any of her career paths primarily because she lacks proficiency communicating with competence and confidence. So sad. So frustrating.

GIVING AN ORAL REPORT OR PRESENTING A SPEECH

Are you one of the English teachers who bemoan the fact that you find it a challenge to teach students to give a "good" speech? Like other colleagues in

Oral report or speech presentation?

your school, do you acknowledge that students do well on "oral reports" yet something still is lacking? Speech-giving really is different from giving an oral report. But how?

Ask your students. Start your unit on public speaking querying your savvy learners about what they notice about a good speaker. Surprisingly, they seldom comment on the content of the speech. Instead, they point out aspects of delivery like giving verbal clues to organization patterns, making eye contact, using gestures, rate of speech, clear articulation, varied intonation, and poise. Of course, middle school students or English language learners probably do not use these terms, but what they do identify shows clearly that *how* the report is delivered is the key feature that makes the speech an effective form of communicating.

Therefore, if you expect your students to become effective, capable, and self-assured speakers, it seems only right that you incorporate into your lesson planning opportunities for students to observe and critique good speaking and allot time to write, practice, and present their own speeches. If you incorporate listening and giving courteous, constructive feedback to presentations, you all win. Students will be practicing critical listening skills, and you will have less out-of-class grading to complete alone. Here are ideas to help achieve multiple oral communication goals by watching, listening, writing, speaking, listening, and critiquing speeches.

Ask students to give intentional attention to speakers. Watch television news reporters. Find and show them short video clips of politicians, of sports figures, and of business men and women delivering speeches. Watch an inspirational speaker giving a talk. Websites such as TED Talks and online presentations on a range of topics by an even wider range of speakers make good examples for analysis. With careful screening, you will find inspiring age-appropriate video for use in your classroom.

Urge your students to watch their teachers. Encourage them to note the delivery styles of their imams, pastors, priests, and rabbis. After just a few observations, your student monitors can assemble a list of those characteristics of content, structure, style, and vocal qualities that make oral presentations simple to follow and easy to remember.

These student observers soon realize that giving a speech is more than reading an essay aloud. Speaking is both an oral and visual presentation designed for a specific audience in a specific place for a specific purpose. On close observations, your students soon pick up that oral communicators have more repetition in their speeches, which guides audiences in following, comprehending, and recalling ideas presented.

Effective speakers tend to use shorter, more declarative sentences comprised of vivid verbs, concrete nouns, graphic images, and even vocabulary chosen for its sound and suggestive power. Carefully selected transitions help hold the speech together while keeping the listeners on track with the positions, arguments, and stories being presented in informative, persuasive, and entertaining speeches. Students may recall these signal words from their study of text structures in nonfiction writing.

A thoughtful speaker takes into consideration what the audience sees as it listens. This begins with attire and then use of gestures and physical space. The speakers also practice their speeches often enough to be able to deliver them at a pace that is easy to follow, using pauses, pacing, and volume to attract and retain attention throughout the speech. But first, these speakers consider their reason for speaking. Your task now is to challenge students to pattern effective content, structure, and deliveries that fit their purpose and personal style.

SPEAKING FOR DIFFERENT PURPOSES

Generally, there are four basic reasons for speeches, and during the course of a school year, you can ask students to prepare and present one of each: to inform, to persuade, to entertain, and to commemorate. You do not have to wait to assign oral presentations until the end of the school year with a formal speech unit of three or four weeks, including assignments for analysis of speeches and time in class to complete their presentations. While elements of preparation and practice both are keys to effective public speaking, having given oral presentations throughout the year, students will have personal experience to reflect on when you begin direct instruction about public speaking as a specific genre of writing and speaking.

The informative speech could be on what students learn about an author, a scientific discovery, or an event in history. A persuasive speech can be preparation for one of the service club speech contests like those of the Rotary and Optimists Club or simply to convince their classmates to read a particular book or to change a belief or behavior about a current event on campus, in the community, or in the world.

To help students relax giving the speech, you could give them the option to present the speech in the persona of a character from a piece of literature or person from history. In fact, the persuasive speech assignment could be to persuade a character in one of the short stories to read the book the student has just finished! The speech to commemorate could be one honoring a special friend, family member, community leader, person in history, or literary character. These commemorative speeches could be solemn and serious or entertaining and humorous but always in good taste.

Check speech language for audience and purpose

PICKING A TOPIC AND PLANNING A SPEECH

You may design a news-related speech assignment for which students think critically about authentic purposes for persuasive speaking and then conduct research and then using correct citation and documentation write and present a speech on that current issue. In this case, too, you can link the assignment to a piece of literature you are studying. For example, you could ask the students to select a current news-related topic that might interest one of the characters from a novel or article the class has read or is studying. Or write a speech to address a problem in the school or community. See chapter 6 for building arguments that lead to persuasion.

CONSTRUCTING THE SPEECH

Your future orators now recognize that writing to speak is very different from simply writing an essay and reading it aloud. So vital to your planning is allotting time for students to construct the speech and practice it. They can focus on revising their draft to have shorter, less complex sentences that flow when they speak them.

Students can check to confirm their manuscript states the goal or position, illustrates with examples, explains it, and reviews that position statement in much the way they used PIE (Position, Illustrate, Explain) patterns in class discussion and other writing assignments. As speakers, they are responsible not only for letting their audience know what the speech is about using some kind of verbalized sign post but also for providing transitions to help the listeners process the information and stay on track.

Your particularly astute students may even recall and apply what they learned in the poetry unit about choosing and arranging words based on their sound and suggestive power, rhythm, and repetition. You can further reduce anxiety by sharing with your prospective orators self-check questions about introducing their topics as well as including various kinds of explanations and supporting evidence that lead to more successful speeches.

STARTING AND DEVELOPING SPEECHES

An effective speech begins well, inviting the audience to listen for a specific purpose, and then is developed with a variety of evidence that appeals to the head, the heart, and often the pocket. Whether one is speaking to inform, argue or persuade, entertain or commemorate the structure of the speech must

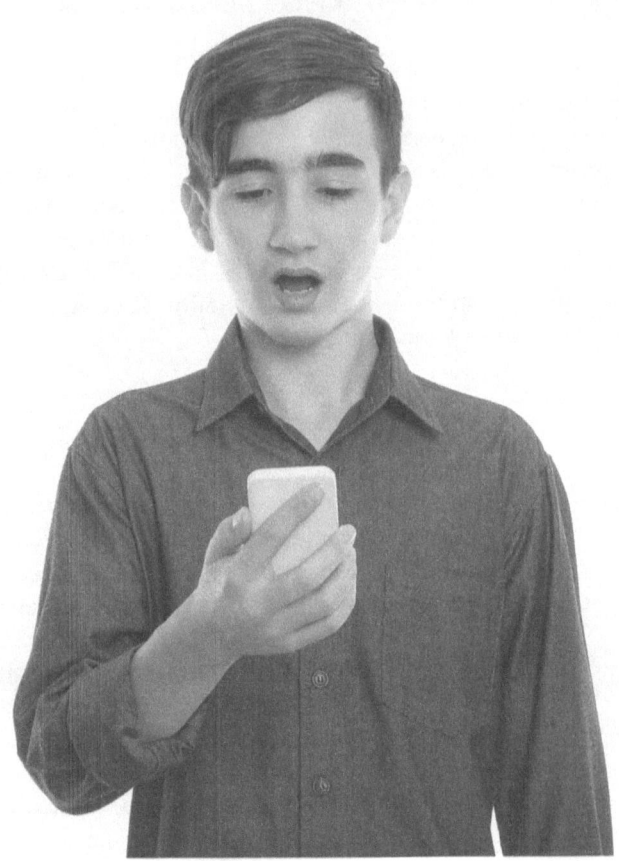

Some students may record on phone when practicing

be considered carefully to be effective. Here are questions students can ask of themselves and their peers as they plan:

1. Does this speech open with an attention getter that will intrigue the audience to listen?
2. Does the introduction include *sign posts* (transitions or signal words) that will indicate the order of the arguments to follow? (See reference to signal words in chapter 5.)
3. Does this speech clearly show that this topic is important to me (personally or as the character)?
4. Does this speech clearly show why this topic is important to the members of my audience?

5. Do I provide adequate support for each main section of my speech? (Write the number of times you include each of these supporting materials in your manuscript.)

   _____illustrations/examples _____explanations
   _____definitions   _____restatements
   _____statistics/numbers   _____humor
   _____comparison/contrast   _____opinion of experts
   _____testimony   _____quotations

6. Does the speech include signal words (transitions) that show the relationship between and among ideas?

Having the students write a script of their speech is a practical way to have them practice the grammar they have been learning, too. Their goal is to communicate clearly in both writing and speaking in an appropriate grammar, Standard English or otherwise. Their choice of grammar and vocabulary makes the difference in how well they get their ideas across to their audience

Presenting in triads can reduce angst

even if their purpose is to entertain peers in their class commemorating a character in a story, a historical figure in history, a real friend, or family member.

VIEW AND CRITIQUE PUBLIC SPEAKERS

An effective method in class assignment is to show students videos of public speakers and invite them to critique what they see based on the criteria to be used when the students present their writing as a speech. Check online sources for speeches of five to seven minutes. Show the entire speech. Have students use the criteria on their class rubrics to indicate on a scale of 1–5 how effective the speech was that they saw. Then, replay the speech, this time turning off the volume, and have students observe the mannerisms, gestures, use of space, and visual aids. Fewer lessons reveal clearer the dual nature of public speaking. See the companion website for this book, www.teachingenglishlanguagearts.com, for sample grading and peer feedback forms to assess speech presentations given in your classes.

PRACTICING, PRACTICING, PRACTICING

Insist that your students get feedback on their speech presentation before giving them in class for evaluation. This listener could be a friend or family member, or, if that is not reasonable to expect in the setting where you teach, this someone could be a classmate. Practicing aloud is the only way for students to know for certain they are familiar enough with content of their speech to deliver it with confidence, making eye contact, using gestures, pronouncing words correctly and clearly, varying the pace of speaking, and maintaining their poise within the time allotted for the speech.

Students sometimes wonder what they should be paying attention to when they practice a speech. Therefore, plan on providing a few guidelines to assure these soon-to-be orators that they are on the right track with their fully developed speech of three or four minutes. Strongly suggest that they time themselves as they give their speech at least three times standing in front of a mirror, holding their notes on the same index cards they plan to use when they give their speech in public.

If they can look up at themselves and keep talking through their speech, they probably are prepared to look up and make more frequent eye contact with their audience. The index cards should have key words and few full sentences. Otherwise the student speaker will be tempted to read rather than talk to the audience. Some students may opt to use their phones. Remind them to have written note cards as backup.

Gestures reinforce ideas

Encourage your students to wear something special on the day they give the speech, an outfit that is especially neat, comfortable, and appropriate for their intended audience. Choosing what to wear reminds them that people in an audience are spectators, also influenced by the speaker's physical appearance and posture. When resources are available at home or at school, recommend that your students make an audio or video recording and listen and watch to hear and see what others are to hear and see when they deliver their speeches.

EVALUATING SPEECHES

Since public speaking is both an oral and visual way of communicating, the criteria used to assess student presentation should take into consideration both elements. Share with your students the criteria you will use to measure their progress. Include features like content and organization and also articulation and pacing and effective use of gestures as well as incorporation of visual aids that support, not distract from, their presentations.

Providing students with probing questions helps them evaluate their speech plans and encourages them to modify them before presenting to the public. For example, if you assign a speech to persuade, ask students to include arguments with a range of appeals.

- Does this speech make appeals to the head (definitions, statistics, explanations, and comparison/contrast)?
- Does this speech make appeals to the heart (humor, explanation, illustrations, quotations, testimony or stories about real people)?
- Does this speech make appeals to the pocket (definitions, facts, statistics, and comparison/contrast related to money)?
- Does the speaker speak clearly, varying the pace to allow time for audience to absorb ideas, and use gestures and visual aids that reinforce and expand audience understanding?

See table 10.1 for chart organizing speaking days and student feedback ideas. Students sign up in color groups of five speakers; one color group speaks each day.

Table 10.1. Speaking Schedule and Feedback Chart

Each group is assigned to comment on one aspect of speech delivery each day, except the day members are scheduled to give their speech.

Day	Red	Green	Purple	Orange	Blue
1	**SPEAKING** (NO FEEDBACK)	Comment on **CONTENT** (Appropriate for audience, variety of support, appeals, quality of evidence and resources, sources cited, etc.)	Comment on **ORGANIZATION** (Introduction with SIGN POST (statement of purpose)) TRANSITIONS (appropriate for kind of speech) CONCLUSION (summary, reflection, or projection without introducing new ideas)	Comment on **VOCAL ISSUES** (Articulation, intonation, pace, pauses, volume, etc.)	Comment on **APPEARANCE** (Appropriate gestures, use of physical space, visual aids, etc.)
2	APPEARANCE	**SPEAKING**	CONTENT	ORGANIZATION	VOCAL ISSUES
3	VOCAL ISSUES	APPEARANCE	**SPEAKING**	CONTENT	ORGANIZATION
4	ORGANIZATION	VOCAL ISSUES	APPEARANCE	**SPEAKING**	CONTENT
5	CONTENT	ORGANIZATION	VOCAL ISSUES	APPEARANCE	**SPEAKING**

Encouragement goes a long way

CONCLUSION

Students who are asked to give a little more attention to observing; assigned to point out the qualities of a good speech presentation; and given time to research, write, and practice become attuned to differences in effectiveness. These young communicators no longer are content simply to give a report but endeavor to present a speech. They will not be tempted to self-muzzle like my friend but become eager and able to develop writing and speaking skills that help them communicate more successfully in any setting.

NOTE

1. Clella Jaffe, "Introduction to Public Speaking and Culture." In *Public Speaking: Concepts and Skills for a Diverse Society*, edited by Jaime Perkins, Renee Deljon, John Gahbauer, 5th ed. (Belmont, CA: Wadsworth/Thomas Learning, 2007), 6.

Afterword

> Education is the passport to the future,
> for tomorrow belongs to those who prepare for it today.
>
> —Malcolm X[1]

Dear reader and colleague, you have both honor and responsibility. After all, you are a professional entrusted with the lives and learning of the students assigned to you. At first, the ups and downs on the way may seem an endless trek up a curvaceous mountain road. But, as you focus on growth, not grades, progress, not speed, you can safely traverse the rolling hills and reach the journey's end triumphantly.

Just steer steadily forward, accelerating and slowing down as the needs arise. Yes, you may creep and climb up some of those steeper hills and may sometimes need to slow down and bumble across pot holes created by inclement weather or natural disasters beyond your control. Rest assured; others have traveled the roads before you and you can make it, too.

Share the driving, listen to back seat drivers, but resist relinquishing control. Pay attention to road signs pointing to the progress you are making together. Do remember to stop regularly to refuel, maximize incidental side trips that can enrich the spirit and inspire the soul, but quickly return to the main path, keeping your eyes on the goal. As you design lessons that respect what each student brings and challenges each one to build on that knowledge and experience, success is assured for you all.

With a firm hand on the wheel, visualizing a mental map of the course, you can safely negotiate the school year and reach your shared destination, all of you wiser and more confident writers than when the expedition first began.

Plan carefully and enjoy the journey

NOTE

1. "Malcolm X," *Brainy Quotes*. https://www.brainyquote.com/quotes/malcolm_x_386475 (accessed June 29, 2018).

Bibliography

"Adolescent Brain Development." *ACT for Youth* 2002. A collaboration of Cornell University, University of Rochester, and the NYS Center for School Safety Upstate Center of Excellence, May. http://www.actforyouth.net/resources/rf/rf_brain_0502.pdf (accessed April 21, 2018).

Bacon, Francis. "Essays of Francis Bacon—Of Studies," Authorama Public Domain Books. http://www.authorama.com/essays-of-francis-bacon-50.html (accessed March 8, 2012).

Blair, Walter, and John Gerber. Eds. *Better Reading Two: Literature*, 3rd ed. Chicago: Scott Foresman and Company, 1959.

Cooley, Mason. "Mason Cooley Quotes," *Brainy Quotes*. http://www.brainyquote.com/quotes/quotes/m/masoncoole396165.html (accessed June 29, 2018).

Daniels, Harvey, and Steven Zememan. "Conferences: The Core of the Workshop." In *Teaching the Best Practice Way: Methods That Matter, K-12*, edited by Harvey Daniels and Marilyn Bazaar p. 184. Portland, ME: Stenhouse Press, 2005.

Ellison, Ralph. "Hidden Name and Complex Fate." In *African-American Literature*, 241–55. Lincolnwood, IL: NTC Publishers, 1998.

"English Language Arts Standards 'Anchor Standards' College and Career Readiness Anchor Standards for Writing." http://www.corestandards.org/ELA-Literacy/CCRA/W/8/ (accessed January 1, 2018).

Epstein, Joseph. "The Personal Essay: A Form of Discovery." In *The Norton Book of Personal Essays*, edited by Joseph Epstein, p. 15. New York: Norton, 1997.

Estrada Ignacio 'Nacho.' Think Exist, Quotes. http://thinkexist.com/quotes/ignacio_estrada/ (accessed June 29, 2018).

Franklin, Benjamin. "Mind Quotes," *Finest Quotes*. http://izquotes.com/quote/283028 (accessed January 2, 2018).

Genevieve, Nancy. American Religion and Literature Society Newsletter, Deshae Lott, Ed. (Spring 2007).

Genevieve, Nancy. *NYX: Daughter of Chaos*. Eureka, IL: NOX Press, 2002.

Genevieve, Nancy. *NYX: Mother of Light*. Eureka, IL: NOX Press, 2001, and ELM. Vol. 5, No. 2, Spring 1997.

Hammerstein, Oscar. "Getting to Know You," Sound Track Lyrics. http://www.stlyrics.com/lyrics/thekingandi/gettingtoknowyou.htm (accessed June 29, 2018).

Hansen, Heather. "Speak English Clearly and Grammatically, and Boost Your Success!" Articles Base. www.articlesbase.com/communication-articles/speak-english-clearly-and-grammatically-and-boost-your-success-195745.html (accessed September 8, 2009).

Houghton-Mifflin College Dictionary. Boston, MA: Houghton Mifflin, 1986.

Hubble, Jeremy. "Here We Are Now, Entertain Us: Poe's Contributions to the Short Story," Jeremy Hubble, April 7, 1996. http://geocities.jeremyhubble.com/poe.html (accessed June 29, 2018).

Jaffe, Clella. "Introduction to Public Speaking and Culture." In *Public Speaking: Concepts and Skills for a Diverse Society*, 5th ed., edited by Jaime Perkins, Renee Deljon, John Gahbauer. Boston: Wadsworth, 2007.

Lear, Edward. n.d. *Poem Hunter*. Accessed October 1, 2018. https://www.poemhunter.com/poem/there-was-an-old-man-in-a-tree/.

Mackenzie, Jock. *Essay Writing: Teaching the Basics from the Ground Up*. Pembroke, NH: Pembroke Publishers, 2007.

"Malcolm X." *Brainy Quotes*. https://www.brainyquote.com/quotes/malcolm_x_386475 (accessed June 29, 2018).

Moberg, Goran. *Critical Literacy and the Aesthetic: Transforming the English Classroom*. New York: The Writing Consultant, 1984.

Pascal, Blaise. *Brainy Quotes*. https://www.brainyquote.com/quotes/blaise_pascal_133403 (accessed June 28, 2018).

Roseboro, Anna J. Small. "Professional and Personal Lives." *California English* 16, no. 1 (September 2010): 8–9.

Rostand, Edmond. *Cyrano de Bergerac*. Lowell Blair, tr. In *World Literature*. Lake Forest, IL: Glencoe MacMillan/McGraw Hill, 1992.

"Standards for Math Practice." *Common Core State Standards Implementation*, 2012. http://www.corestandards.org/Math/Content/8/introduction (accessed June 29, 2018).

Troupe, Quincy. "My Poems Have Holes Sewn into Them." In *Transcircularities: New and Selected Poems*, 1st ed., edited by Quincy Troupe, 98–99. Minneapolis, MN: Coffee House Press, 2002.

Twain, Mark. From chapter 17 of *The Adventures of Huckleberry Finn* https://contentserver.adobe.com/store/books/HuckFinn.pdf (accessed 28 September 2018)

Urquhart, Vicki. "Using Writing in Math to Deepen Student Learning," *ERIC Collection*. https://eric.ed.gov/?id=ED544239 (accessed June 29, 2018).

Ward, William Arthur. "Quotes about Teaching," National Education Association, 2012. https://www.brainyquote.com/quotes/william_arthur_ward_103463 (accessed April 21, 2018).

About the Author

Anna J. Small Roseboro, a National Board Certified Teacher, has over four decades' experience teaching in public and private schools, mentoring early career educators, and facilitating leadership institutes. She was awarded Distinguished Service Awards by the California Association of Teachers of English (2009) and the National Council of Teachers of English (2016).

Roseboro earned a BA in speech communications from Wayne State University and an MA in curriculum design from the University of California, San Diego. Her research investigated the link between writing to learn and retention in mathematics. She earned the Early Adolescent/English Language Arts Certificate from the National Board for Professional Teaching Standards in 1998.

Roseboro represented Rotary International in a group-study exchange with educators in East Africa. In addition to teaching young adolescents in Michigan, Missouri, New York, Massachusetts, and California, she has taught adults at the Rochester Theological Institute, at Grand Valley State University and Calvin College.

Roseboro served sixteen years as director of summer session programs for students in grades five through twelve, coached a National Forensic League competitive speech team for twelve years, and was English Department chair from 1999 through 2005 at the Bishop's School. During 2008–2009, Anna was a faculty leader at the NCTE Affiliate and Leadership Conference and served as master teacher for the San Francisco Bay Area Teachers Center in an online teaching environment.

Roseboro's articles have appeared in the *English Journal*, *English Leadership Quarterly*, *Fine Lines: A National Quarterly Creative Writing Journal*, and *California English*. She has published three texts for teachers—*Teaching Middle School Language Arts* (2010), *Teaching Writing in the Middle School* (2013), and *Teaching Reading in the Middle School* (2013)—a novel, and a poetry book for young people. Her writing appears in online professional blogs, in online communities for teachers such as English Companion and the Teaching and Learning Forum, and in *Continuing the Journey: Becoming a Better Teacher of Literature and Informational Texts* (2017).

Now retired from full-time teaching, Anna J. Small Roseboro serves as codirector of the Conference on English Education Commission to Support Early Career English Language Arts Teachers and of the National Council of Teachers of English Early Career Educators of Color Leadership Award Program. She makes her home in Western Michigan with her husband of five decades.

www.ingramcontent.com/pod-product-compliance
Lightning Source LLC
Chambersburg PA
CBHW021851300426
44115CB00005B/109